2-IN-1
THE EFFECTIVE
PROJECT
LEADER

*Discover Success Principles
for a Project Manager
& Apply Best Project
Management Practices*

© Copyright Ready Set Agile! 2021 - All rights reserved.

The content contained within this book may not be reproduced, duplicated, or transmitted without direct written permission from the author or the publisher except for the use of brief quotations in a book review. Under no circumstances will any blame or legal responsibility be held against the publisher, or author, for any damages, reparation, or monetary loss due to the information contained within this book. Either directly or indirectly. You are responsible for your own choices, actions, and results.

Legal Notice:
This book is copyright protected. This book is only for personal use. You cannot amend, distribute, sell, use, quote or paraphrase any part, or the content within this book, without the consent of the author or publisher except for the use of brief quotations in a book review.

Disclaimer notice:
Please note the information contained within this book is for educational and entertainment purposes only. All effort has been executed to present accurate, up to date, and reliable, complete information. No warranties of any kind are declared or implied. Readers acknowledge that the author is not engaging in the rendering of legal, financial, medical, or professional advice. The content within this book has been derived from various sources. Please consult a licensed professional before attempting any techniques outlined in this book.
By reading this book, the reader agrees that under no circumstances is the author responsible for any losses, direct or indirect, which are incurred as a result of the use of the information contained within this book, including, but not limited to,—errors, omissions, or inaccuracies.

2-IN-1
THE EFFECTIVE PROJECT LEADER

Discover Success Principles for a Project Manager & Apply Best Project Management Practices

2021

TABLE OF CONTENTS

- 11 **INTRODUCTION**
- 17 **CHAPTER 1** The Beginning of an Effective Project Manager
- 35 **CHAPTER 2** Key Project Components and Their Associated Skills
- 49 **CHAPTER 3** What Is Competency in Project Management Really About?
- 59 **CHAPTER 4** Outside the Petri Dish: Management Culture and Organizational Behavior
- 81 **CHAPTER 5** Project Sponsors: The Keys to the Project Management Kingdom
- 93 **CHAPTER 6** Always Be Closing
- 103 **CHAPTER 7** Take Command of the Technical Skills
- 117 **CHAPTER 8** Level Up Your PM Game
- 131 **CHAPTER 9** Always Be Improving
- 145 **FINAL WORDS**
- 150 **REFERENCES**
- 153 **GLOSSARY AND ABBREVIATIONS**

- 157 **INTRODUCTION**
- 163 **CHAPTER 1** Introduction to Leadership
- 181 **CHAPTER 2** Got a Problem?
- 197 **CHAPTER 3** Fight! Learn to Love the Conflict You're In
- 211 **CHAPTER 4** There Is No "I" in Team
- 231 **CHAPTER 5** Put Me In, Coach, I'm Ready To Play
- 253 **CHAPTER 6** Level Up Your Best
- 269 **CHAPTER 7** Serve for Success
- 277 **CHAPTER 8** What We Have Here Is a Failure to Communicate
- 291 **CHAPTER 9** HECG Secret for Success
- 299 **FINAL WORDS**
- 302 **REFERENCES**
- 305 **GLOSSARY AND ABBREVIATIONS**
- 307 **LEAVE A REVIEW**
- 309 **MY OTHER BOOKS YOU WILL LOVE**

TWO BONUS CHECKLISTS

NEGOTIATION
Stages – Guidelines – Techniques

- Negotiation Styles
- Winning Practices
- Becoming a master negotiator

GETTING SUPPORT

from the
- ✓ Management
- ✓ Sponsor
- ✓ Stakeholders

- Triple Your Chances for the Project's Success
- 13 Tips on Getting Support

To download your checklist, click and visit the link:

rsagile.activehosted.com/f/21

BONUS: 7 BEST PRACTICES CHECKLIST

BEING AN EFFECTIVE PROJECT MANAGER

Your Guide to Becoming a Project Management Rock Star: Best Practices, Methodology, and Success Principles for a Project Leader

INTRODUCTION

AS a project manager, you're used to juggling tasks, people, and resources, all while keeping the client happy. But, do you ever wish it were easier? That you and your team could do more with all those work hours you're given? Sometimes, it's a slog to get everything and everyone on the same page and all working together as one team to achieve the project goal.

Maybe you've been struggling to ensure that projects are completed on time and budget. You may think you've estimated the resource needs correctly, and then there's suddenly an unexpected and unforeseen development that ends up destroying the timeline. As of the time of writing this book (June 2020), we're still in the middle of the coronavirus epidemic. No one saw this coming, and it has upset the business plans for quite a few project managers.

No one can reasonably blame you for not seeing the COVID-19 virus coming beforehand. However, do you find that you're often held accountable for issues that are out of your control? As the project manager (PM), *you* are the one who's responsible for the completion of the project as planned. Despite this, project teams or stakeholders may sometimes seem to take it too far and blame you for things that genuinely were not in your control.

Stakeholders are known for pressuring their project managers and teams. Other issues may have come up, and they'd like to shift some of the budget they agreed to invest in the project somewhere else. And they may want you to finish ahead of time, despite signing off on the months of work that you estimated the project would take. Maybe they want to add some additional features to the scope without increasing the budgets for time and money appropriately.

Staying organized in terms of time can also be difficult for a PM. Once the schedule starts to slip, it's not always easy to get it back where it needs to be. You're also responsible for organizing the work, and some tasks must be completed before the next one begins, which may cause headaches when your resources aren't available as expected. How can those tasks be completed effectively, so the project moves on to the next phase in time?

Did any of these issues resonate with you? If so, you've come to the right place! This book is intended for project managers to elevate their game and create solutions for their problems. You'll learn key elements of being a project manager, along with step-by-step methods for improving in the areas where you need help. Some of these are based on leadership fundamentals, like communication and collaboration; others are focused on the technical skills required for the project's management.

This book is not necessarily about the technical skills that your team members will bring along with them, though you will see me promoting the idea of learning the basics of a project team's tasks. We will be discussing more about the skills specific to management and not the underlying functional knowledge that your team players will bring.

In addition to benefiting you as a PM, how does knowing how to be an effective project manager help others? Being effective is a huge part of making the project successful. You're more likely to bring projects in on time and at the expected costs, which makes you more likely to complete the project successfully and satisfy the stakeholders. Your effectiveness means that their expectations have been met, and they're pleased with the results you delivered.

Your absorption of this material is also to the advantage of your project team(s). When you're doing your job well, they're freed up to do their best work as well. If the environment you provide them is healthy, their morale will be higher, and they will be more productive and willing to go the extra mile for you.

When you, as the PM, understand where you should prioritize your work, look out for potential threats to project completion that are looming on the horizon, and how best to communicate with all those

involved on the project. If you do so, everyone will be happier with the results.

Being more effective on your projects has personal benefits for you as a PM. Project managers who can bring in projects consistently and according to schedule and budget are rock stars in the project management world. Clients will want to hire you because they will notice your successful track record. Besides, you'll enjoy your work more since the daily tasks won't seem so difficult. Once you can get the project onto a consistent schedule, and all the team members and stakeholders are moving in the same direction, projects won't be as difficult to complete. You can then enjoy yourself and still get an excellent job done.

Effective PMs can remove a lot of pressure. You'll still probably run into your share of stakeholders who just want to squeeze what they believe is a quick upgrade into your meticulously constructed framework. However, once everyone is on your side, there will be much less external pressure, and clients will be more willing to give you the benefit of the doubt.

The more projects you work on, the more you can boost your career. New projects mean a wealth of lessons and experiences that will multiply your level of expertise exponentially. I'll show you how to spot these ideas and leverage them to your own benefit.

Finally, you'll develop winning teams that are rock stars in project management. They'll want to work with you in the future because an effective PM leads their team in a way that makes it a joy to work on projects. They will also, naturally, give their best in return. They'll respect you, not only for your success, but also for understanding their jobs and how you let them work most effectively. We know that people are happier at work when they have some control over it, so to the extent you can empower team members to accomplish their jobs, the better it will be for their morale.

At this point, you're probably wondering how I can be so sure about the results of effective project managers! I've participated in projects and been a PM myself in many different project management positions. I've collaborated on a variety of projects, from small start-ups to large, cross-divisional ones with huge budgets and a timeline of several years. In my career, I've seen projects succeed, and I've also seen them fail. My goal is to help aspiring PMs learn how to be effective quickly without spending years learning it on the ground as I did. Throughout all my years of project management, I've learned vital lessons on how to be an effective project manager, and I want to share this with as many PMs as I possibly can.

By using my experience and knowledge, you'll learn the key elements of project management and how to improve in the areas where you don't feel as confident. You'll understand how to win over the sponsors of your project and have them cheering you and the team on while removing any impediments that they have influence over. You'll have the keys to executing the plan, technical skills, and knowledge of project management as a business. In addition, you'll learn the basics of the most important project management (and life) skill: continuous improvement.

Many other PMs, just like you, have used these principles to build better lives for themselves. Being an effective project manager often leads to personal improvement as well. After understanding and implementing the material that I've gathered for you here in this one place, they've gone on to lead successful projects. Such is all just from the simple steps that have been outlined in this book.

Many PMs weren't sure they were really cut out to be rock stars, but after becoming more effective, they went from zero to hero pretty quickly. For me, some of these transformations were a little short of miraculous. Not only did the lessons benefit them, but their entire team and other stakeholders reaped the benefits too.

Why wait to have a career that's fun again? One where you don't have to work harder, but just a little smarter to get to where you want to go? If you're already a project manager and you feel like you're struggling through your workdays, don't hold off on reading this book. Start making your work life a little easier by increasing your effectiveness today.

Effective project management at work is great, but it also spills over into your personal life. For one thing, you're not trying to roll the ball uphill, so you have more time for family and friends. When you get more organized in one aspect of your life, you will tend to take that skill into all the others too. As you improve your communication with stakeholders and team members, you will become more effective at home as well. You'll initiate and complete personal projects to good results, and your ability to hire and deal with the right specialists to make your projects successful will increase.

You may be wondering—what exactly does *effective* mean when it comes to project management? It's about achieving common goals with given resources in terms of money and time. It also entitles becoming a skilled prioritizer who can focus on the work and deliver and creating value for the business through the successful completion of the project. It means you do the work faster and smarter, take your projects further, and—most importantly—enjoying the work that you do.

Sound good? Let's get effective!

CHAPTER 1

THE BEGINNING OF AN EFFECTIVE PROJECT MANAGER

THIS book is for anyone who wants to be the most effective project manager (PM) they can be. That is whether you're already a project manager looking to level up, or you're still aspiring to become one. Here, you'll discover what you need to know, so you can hit the ground running right after reading and practicing the tips in this book.

What, then, makes a good project manager? It's not the title, position, education, nor experience, although these elements can help tremendously. It's something within you. Let's discover this something together.

What is the Role of a Project Manager?

Roughly speaking, a project is a group of tasks that must be performed to achieve a specific outcome, whether that be something new or improved. This can be a project that you fulfill at home, such as renovating your house, or at your work. Projects can be found in all industries, including software, manufacturing, and financial services. Any department within a company can manage a project to improve the current process or deliver a new product. Project complexity can range from fairly simple with few tasks to extremely complex, and they could require just one team or significantly more.

No matter what type of project you're considering, there has to be someone to oversee the entire process, and that person is the project manager. Titles may vary in the agile project management world; for example, a Six Sigma team might be led by a Black Belt or Master Black Belt, and a Scrum team could be led by a Scrum master, (see my previous book *Become an Agile Project Manager* for more details on these kinds of positions).

In the world of traditional (or "waterfall") project management, the PM would keep a tight hold on the reins. They typically negotiate with the client representatives, develop the budget, hire the team, organize the tasks, and create the schedule. It's a top-down style of management that works for projects that have specific delivery dates and where one task cannot be started before the previous one is completed.

Agile project management teams, by contrast, are self-organizing and all the team members are involved in client communication, budgeting, and figuring out which tasks should be performed next. Agile teams have a system in place (known as the artifacts) that permit them to keep track of what is required, has been accomplished, and needs to occur next. These projects are run in short sprints or iterations, so the teams would manage their own

schedules. Agile is better for projects that may require quick adaptation to changing circumstances, such as software development.

Whichever project management type you're using, there's a need for someone to keep an eye on the entirety of the project. There are several characteristics and skills that a PM needs to be effective for any project, which are a combination of technical and leadership skills.

- **Prioritization**

    There are always enough tasks to fill up 25 hours of your 24-hour day. Not all of them are important or necessary, and some you may be able to ignore altogether. To be a successful PM, you need to determine what's most important for your team to accomplish in the next time period (day, week, etc.). Once that is done, move to the next, then the next. Besides, you'll probably need to help your team prioritize their own tasks.

    Do the right thing at the right time.

- **Organization**

    The role of a project manager involves juggling a lot of different tasks and concepts, with plenty of minutiae and distractions. If you're not organized, you'll be snowed under the high volume of work.

    Two main ideas contribute to being well-organized—one is having a tidy space, represented by Marie Kondo (n.d.).[1] Your work surfaces should be neat when you arrive, so you're not distracted by the mess. Everything that you need for your work needs a home, and everything that's not necessary should be stored for when you need it; otherwise, it should be eliminated if you have no need for it at all.

The other thing you need to organize is your time. Prioritization helps you stay on top of what's urgent and important, and a successful project manager will ensure that their time is productive.

Teamwork

As the PM, it's your responsibility to make sure that the team is working together. Otherwise, you won't be able to make your deadlines, and the project itself could fail. You'll need to mediate conflicts when they arise, remembering that healthy disagreement is positive for the team.

You'll be a player-coach on this one, whether you're working on a traditional or agile project. You're building a team, not just with your own workers, but also with clients, client representatives, vendors, and other stakeholders. As you work with others, you will show your team members more about how it's done.

Communication and diplomacy

Though agile places more emphasis on communication than waterfall does, in both situations being able to connect with other people is a requirement. Your team members may only be talking to each other and the PM, but you have several audiences to check in with. A key function for a PM is to provide understandable and actionable updates to stakeholders, where necessary.

You'll likely be dealing with people from a variety of backgrounds and educational experiences, and all of them need to understand you clearly. In addition, communication can't be offensive or harmful to anyone; it should build relationships rather than damage them.

Hence the importance of diplomacy as a component! Later in this chapter, we'll discuss emotional intelligence and why it's necessary—but for now, just understand that being able to deliver bad news without severing the relationship is key. Projects may go over schedule on time or budget, the team may misunderstand the client and make a mistake, or some other issue rears its ugly head in the middle of the project. Stakeholders need to be informed so they don't become excessively upset or pull the plug.

See the big picture

Ideally, the PM would understand all the different tasks that their team performs. They may not be an expert in any of them, but they would have a working knowledge of what each person specializes in. They're not the ones doing the work necessarily, but they are overseeing it. They're the ones who must see how all the pieces in the puzzle fit together, even if each individual team member only knows what they themselves are working on.

The PM would understand how all the tasks come together to create the deliverable, and what needs to happen before the next task can commence. This also includes what the team and stakeholders need to know about the process, and how to integrate their input into the project. They should perform the research necessary to pull everything together in a puzzle that evolves dynamically.

Fresh perspective

One thing that machines and robots can't do for us is to give us a new perspective on a problem. They can churn through data and create charts and graphs to make the statistics more understandable, but they can't turn the problem on its head to see if they should shake loose some different ideas that way.

The more you (and your team) can be creative, the more viewpoints you will have on the situation, and the more likely you will be able to develop a good solution to the problem.

- **Critical thinking**

    Unfortunately, most of the time, you won't have complete insight into decision making. You may be able to see your options, but you won't be able to project them out into the future with a full guarantee that trying X will work, or that Z will work better. You may not have clarity on all your choices, or you may not have the resources for your first and best option.

    Successful PMs can think through what they know—to paraphrase Donald Rumsfeld, former Secretary of Defense for the United States, the known knowns and the known unknowns to reach a conclusion. They can also analyze the situation when the unknown unknowns show up.

- **Leadership**

    As a PM you're leading the team, and a strong PM inspires and motivates the team. Modern leadership uses emotional intelligence skills to communicate and build relationships and connections. This is particularly with the team, but with others, such as stakeholders, as well.

    You would set the vision; then, you would coach the team to achieve it. You're personally responsible for the success or failure of the project. In other words, you're not a manager who can blameshift up or outwards—you're the leader who goes down with the ship, or reaps the rewards of a well-done project that reaches the objectives.

Project Leader vs. Project Manager

Although the title is *project manager*, a great PM is still a *project leader*. We alluded to it in the previous section, but what does it really mean to lead a project as opposed to merely managing it?

Very briefly, the difference comes down to strategy compared to tactics. A leader is focused on the strategy: the big picture and what needs to be done (at a bird's-eye view) to accomplish the objective. They empower and inspire their team members to help them reach that vision and get the job done.

By contrast, a manager is on the tactical side: figuring out what needs to be done in what order, and who should do what. In this book, we'll be discussing the role of a manager rather than a leader, which will be covered in the second book of this bundle. However, these two roles go hand in hand, and a successful PM has to master both.

In agile, the difference between project management and project leadership is more apparent. Because the teams are self-organizing, they would decide what needs to be done next and in what order. They're usually cross-functional, so they can decide amongst themselves who is responsible for which task and when. The project manager sets the vision and strategy for the project.

In waterfall project management, the PM may act in both roles. At the very beginning, they would decide strategically with the client on the deliverable. They would provide the vision for how the project would work, then persuade the stakeholders to buy into that vision. After that, it's manager mode time as they determine schedules, budgets, and who is responsible for what and when. In this type of project, the entire process is mapped out at the beginning, soup to nuts, which is mostly the PM's role, though they can consult with the team members who have expertise in individual sections.

Leaders need to demonstrate three types of mental competence. A manager may be able to get away with two of the three, but a true leader shows evidence of all of them.

1. IQ and cognitive skills

This is measured by IQ tests and mostly involves problem-solving and analytical skills. It's fixed at birth. Although you can acquire more knowledge, your IQ is relatively static over your lifetime. On the other hand, cognitive skills such as paying attention, retaining memories, and the ability to both plan for and execute the steps necessary to achieve a goal can be improved when you spend time learning and practicing them.

2. Emotional intelligence

Also known as EQ, this type of intelligence is about how well you can build and maintain relationships. People with high EQ are aware of their own emotions and can regulate them. They also help others to manage their emotions.

Unlike IQ, you can increase your EQ merely by applying yourself. Those who work for supervisors with high levels of emotional intelligence are 400% less likely to leave the job (Leadem, 2018).[2] You can see why this aspect is essential for leadership!

3. Managerial intelligence

This type of intelligence (MQ) measures your knowledge of skills and the qualities necessary to manage others (Zilicus, 2014).[3] It's about managing and controlling resources (material and human) and achieving the goal. You can learn this skill as well to improve over time.

A study of these different types of intelligence showed that EQ is most important to the success of a project, contributing 36%; IQ 27%; and managerial intelligence 16% (Dulewicz, et al, 2016).[4] You can see that emotional intelligence is critical for leaders, but there are additional issues that come up for a project manager to be a project leader (for the rest of the book, understand that an effective project manager is also a project leader). One of the aspects of the project that must be managed are the constraints on the project itself.

Triple Constraint Triangle

Don't worry—good knowledge of geometry isn't necessarily required for project managers, effective or otherwise. The Triple Constraint triangle is a way to visualize the boundaries on the project. Those three are the points of the triangle: time, scope, and budget, with quality being the central theme of the triangle. You might also see more recent adaptations that describe constraints as a square, with quality being the fourth point and expectations as the theme of the square.

When you're thinking about your project, you will need to manage all these limitations.

- **Cost**

    Your clients don't have infinite amounts of money to throw at the project you're managing and need to see a good return on their investment. They would allocate a certain amount of money, and it's your job to deliver within that framework. Clients really dislike it when you ask for more money; therefore, in general, the budget you draw up in the beginning should be the maximum you should expect.

- **Time**

    Clients need their projects delivered for a specific deadline. For example, if you're managing a project to develop a new toy, the firm will want the completed project in advance of the end-of-year holiday season to ramp up production, marketing, and sales.

    PMs who deliver projects routinely on time are extremely valuable to their clients. Clients want to know they'll get their result when they were expecting to achieve it. Being able to do so consistently makes a project manager very attractive.

- **Scope**

    Whatever you agreed to deliver must be satisfied by the completion of the project. That also means that both you and the client need to be clear on the scope, which is often where misunderstandings occur.

    For example, if you're working on a software development project, the client may think they've contracted for a fully functioning, tested, and bug-free app. However, the PM may have understood that they're only responsible for a beta version. Ensure that you ask the right questions and the scope is spelled out clearly in the documentation.

- **Quality**

    Clients want deliverables that will stand up to usage. However, some clients may be OK with a version that's closer to beta than full release, in the parlance of software development.

    The project manager must understand the expectations that the clients and stakeholders have in terms of quality, and they're responsible for delivering it. Clients want results—not tick marks on a checklist.

- **Expectations**

    Like scope, expectations are often misunderstood. As a PM, you'll need to ask probing questions to be clear on what it is they think they will receive at the end of the process.

In an ideal world, of course, there are no errors or wrenches thrown into the works. Everyone who was hired to work on the project stays until the bitter end and manages their work so the project can stay exactly within the budget and time constraints. All team members

work to their highest quality, and the deliverable should be of the finest quality possible.

"You can have it fast, cheap, or good—pick two." —Anonymous

In the real world where you'll be operating, the project will not flow smoothly from beginning to end and without bumps in the road or obstacles in the way. The Triple Constraint is about how you shift from one point to another to achieve the best compromise possible when you can't make all three.

For example, once the project starts going over schedule, it's extremely difficult, if not impossible, to get that train back on track and make your deadline. You will have some decisions to make, and, as a PM, you'll be the one held accountable for them. You could allow the project to simply run over the deadline, but the client may not accept this. You could hire more people or other resources to make up the time, but that will put you over budget, unless you gave yourself some wiggle room for exactly these kinds of situations. On the other hand, you could pull back a little on the scope to finish on time, which will decrease the quality.

Often, the client will let you know what's most important to them. They might stress to you that the project needs to be completed within the budget they provided to you and not a penny more. In that case, you may allow the project to continue with fewer resources past the deadline.

There could also be a drop-dead delivery date put in place, in which case, you might propose to hire more resources. If they've given you this kind of guidance, balancing the three constraints may be a little easier because you know what you have to hold steady on and can then figure out how to massage the other two issues to achieve the goal.

When you don't know what's most important, you may have to play with your problem-solving a little bit more. For example, to avoid a complete trainwreck, you may choose to go a little over budget and time and ease up on the scope and quality a little as well. Depending on the project and the client, there may or may not be a clear solution for how to balance these three constraints on your project.

You'll need to communicate your decisions to the team and stakeholders. Depending on the style of project management you're working with (waterfall or agile), both the stakeholders and team may have to be involved in the decision. Ultimately, it's your responsibility and you're the one held accountable, but your team members may come up with a solution you hadn't considered. The stakeholder may be able to squeeze a bit more out of the budget if they understand why you're asking for the additional resources, and they might have some expertise that they can bring to solving the problem as well.

Given that no one—or at least not everyone—will be pleased with the news, your communication skills as a PM will become extremely important in these situations! You need to be direct and clear and not passive and wishy-washy because you won't like delivering bad news. At the same time, everyone must be clear that you respect their opinions and are willing to entertain other ideas and solutions. Involving the client representatives in the decisions themselves will help you get buy-in from the clients. This will assist enormously when you're asking for extensions of time or extra resources. People dislike being told what to do, so as much as they can feel in control, or at least have a voice in the process, the easier the constraint balancing will be for you.

You can also see that the more respect your team has for you, the easier the balancing will be. We'll get into more on how you can inspire and motivate your team members to respect you later in the book.

Jack of All Trades

When you know fundamentally what each of your project workers is doing daily, you will be better able to inspire the respect of the people on your team.

Have you ever worked for a boss whom you felt didn't understand your job? Were you frustrated that they couldn't understand how long certain tasks took because they had no concept of what actually went on during the completion of the task? Did you and your coworkers ever make fun of them behind their backs for being so clueless, or make remarks about how they fulfilled the Peter Principle?

"People tend to rise to the level of their incompetence." –
Dr. Laurence Peter (Wikipedia, 2020)[5]

This suggests that, as people get promoted, they become less effective because doing well in one job doesn't guarantee the same in another.

You don't necessarily have to master each of the skills that your team members have or be able to do their jobs at the drop of a hat. Since most of the time you're also hiring team members, you will need to be able to judge their level of performance. If you have no idea what they're doing and what's involved in their work, you will have no way of understanding who's better at the task than another.

As a project manager, you're the one who fits the puzzle together to complete the project. To do that, you'll need to know the size and shape of the different pieces. When you're managing a software project, for example, not understanding basic programming and data structures means you will have no idea what the shape of the pieces are, thus you won't be able to fit them together logically.

By contrast, when you understand the fundamentals of the tasks that will be performed, you'll also have a clue about how long they take, the kind of skills a person would need to fulfill them, and the resources they would need. Such allows you to view all the pieces clearly and put the puzzle together in a way that best fits the picture you've agreed to deliver to the client. Complete with timelines for each task and team member, and provide allowable expenses for each.

You're Part of the Puzzle Too

Don't forget yourself when you're figuring out how all the pieces work together. Whether your project is waterfall or agile, you'll be encouraging your team members, supporting them in work, keeping an eye on the details, and reminding everyone of the vision that you're trying to achieve. You will need to be a leader—not just a manager of people. The qualities that you model can make or break a successful project, and you'll inspire everyone working on the project to follow your lead.

If you're not very effective and waste a lot of time and energy, so will everyone else. If you promote playing the blame game and avoiding accountability, you'll find that no one on the team will ever be responsible for anything that went wrong. Client representatives may even throw you under the bus when they're talking to their superiors about what went wrong on the project. If you get defensive when others offer criticism, no one on the team will offer up suggestions for improvement. If you can't communicate with people at all levels of the organization, and from all backgrounds and experiences, you'll end up at an impasse when you can't get your message across to the people who need to hear it.

The good news is that you can learn to be an effective PM and avoid all those mistakes. In the rest of this book, you'll discover all the pieces you need so you can deliver the best results. It's not just about

specific roles that you would take on in the project, though they play a role and we'll discuss them in more detail; it's also about leadership skills and how you can improve yours.

The paradigm has shifted away from command-and-control style leadership, in which the PM is infallible and up on a pedestal. Waterfall style project management is more about command and control, and, as such, it's fallen out of favor. It has a rigid structure and planning is done almost entirely at the start of the process, which allows for less freedom and flexibility.

Agile is more successful, and more companies have begun to adopt this faster style that allows them to go to market sooner and reap their return on investment quicker. Similarly, being a project manager is more about encouraging and coaching the team to achieve their goal instead of providing carrot-and-stick incentives.

You'll discover everything you need to know about being an effective project manager and put all the puzzle pieces together to deliver solid and successful projects when reading through this book.

Key Takeaways

Effective project managers understand how to put all the pieces of a project puzzle together to deliver rewarding results and experience for the clients, the team, and themselves.

- Certain qualities, such as good communication, teamwork, and being well-organized, are essential for the effective project manager.

- Project managers who want to be effective and successful need to lead a project strategically; not just manage it in terms of tactics.

- PMs must balance the three constraints of a project—scope, timeframe, and cost—which is visualized by the Triple Constraint triangle.

- A trait that helps project managers balance the triangle is to be a jack of all trades, in which they would have a fundamental understanding of all the tasks that need to be accomplished.

- The project manager is the one who fits pieces of the puzzle together.

- Anyone can learn how to be a more effective PM.

In the next chapter, you will learn about the key components for a successful project.

---

[1] https://shop.konmari.com/pages/about
[2] https://www.entrepreneur.com/article/318187
[3] http://zilicus.com/Resources/blog-2014/Project-Leadership-Or-Project-Management-Becoming-Effective-Project-Leader-Part-ii.html
[4] http://doi.org/10.4236/ajibm.2016.64043
[5] https://en.wikipedia.org/wiki/Peter_principle

CHAPTER 2

KEY PROJECT COMPONENTS AND THEIR ASSOCIATED SKILLS

AREN'T all the aspects of a project important? Well, yes and no. There are a few parts of a project that have a much larger effect on the success—or lack thereof—compared to others. This is true whether you're managing an agile project or a traditional one. If you can get these significant components right, you'll set yourself up well for success. Projects tend to fail because the following aspects weren't properly planned or communicated.

Scope

In the first chapter, you learned that it's common for the scope to be misunderstood between the project manager and the client. However, just because it's common doesn't mean that PMs shouldn't avoid this confusion whenever possible.

One of the major malfunctions in defining the features of the product or process to be delivered is known as "scope creep." That is, the project management team or client adds on to the original features of the project. Once the scope is broader than what was originally promised, the timeline or the budget, or both, will be put under sudden pressure. Scope creep can affect the quality as well. The higher number of elements added, the more the entire project may degrade in quality.

It's important to know that, often, scope creep doesn't happen all at once. Sometimes, the client may ask for something extra at first, and then they seem to forget it wasn't included in the original scope, timeline, and budget. Clients ask for additional features mostly because they may not have been sure what they want exactly in the beginning. If the client is unclear at first, then the team may not gather enough information for the requirements analysis. Without truly understanding what the client wants, it becomes easy to continue adding new details as the client asks for them.

Ultimately, the PM is responsible for ensuring that scope creep doesn't happen on their watch! Making sure the requirements analysis is sufficient is one task that they oversee. There are also many reasons not necessarily related to the client that can be responsible for scope creep, depending on the circumstances.

- **A project that has never been done before**

    If it's a new project, or the PM and team are new to the project type, they may not realize the complexity of it initially. If no one on the team has that much experience in the subject, there will be no one to ask and no use cases to examine from previous projects to apply as a reference.

    When that's the case, it's best if the PM expects cost and time overruns and budgets accordingly. It's highly unlikely that the project will be less work than you expected. Assume it will be

more and ensure that you have some contingency planning in place to deal with extra complexity as it arises.

If those types of projects have been successful (or not) in the past, a smart PM will study those use cases to decide the timeline and budget required to manage it successfully.

- **Analysis paralysis**

    Studying and researching, in so many ways, is so much easier than actually entering production! You don't have to take responsibility for anything going wrong while you're researching the problem. With all this information overload in the world, it's incredibly easy to go down the rabbit hole and never get anything done. After all, you could spend an evening easily reading all the articles about scope creep on the Internet! You may only get started when the deadline is looming and you're starting to panic.

    Analysis paralysis is especially common among perfectionists. They find it difficult when they start on production that does not yield perfect results at first, and they prefer to continue analyzing instead of working. Once they *do* get started, they may be reluctant to ship or send their piece of work for testing because it isn't perfect yet.

    "Done is better than perfect." —Anonymous

    Workers downstream from the perfectionist often get very frustrated because they don't have what they need to do their own jobs until the perfectionist finishes theirs. It is much better for the work to be released on time, so the rest of the team can perform their work. If you wait for perfection, you may never have any product at all. There's always a tweak that could be made or a little touch-up, but the product needs to be released at some point.

- **No control over changes**

    If the PM doesn't take the reins of making changes to the scope, the project is much more likely to be a victim of scope creep. Instead, the PM should include upfront documentation that any scope changes must go through an approval process. When the client can't drop in on the team members and request a change, they'll give it more thought. The PM can also specify in the documentation that extra time and costs for the change must be approved, so the client is aware of the consequences of their request.

Overcommitment by the PM

As discussed in the previous chapter, although, as a project manager, you may have a basic knowledge of the various tasks and skill sets required for the project, you may not know enough about the learning domain to estimate its scope accurately.

Never make a commitment to the client regarding a function you're not well experienced in without consulting your team members, who are the experts in their domain. Only after they've given you the approval on a reasonable timeframe can you go to the client and make that agreement.

Not getting users involved early

This issue is particularly important when it comes to software development. The client representative, if they're in management, may not have understood what exactly the users need. In agile project management, users are involved as part of the process, but that isn't often the case in waterfall.

They need to be involved from the *beginning*—not just toward the end when the team delivers the product. If they're brought into the process late and the project isn't providing what they need, the scope must be changed (with its deadlines and expenses) to ensure that the team delivers something that is valuable to the users.

The users provide valuable feedback to the team on what's working and what isn't. When done early enough in the project, changes can be made that won't necessarily disrupt the timeframe or budget.

- **Gold plating**

    Sometimes, the team members will add to the project believing that they are creating more value, which is known as gold plating. It's common in software development, but not exclusive to that industry. The changes they make don't necessarily add any value to the project, especially if they're not communicating regularly with the users. The gold plating eats up time and money without guaranteeing client satisfaction.

    It's not relevant whether the team thinks it has created value; the key metric is whether the client believes they did.

Value

The project is initiated to create value for the business or client. Keeping that at the forefront of their minds in terms of the goals and daily work will help the project management team supervise the scope.

Creating a deliverable of value is a matter of pride and accomplishment for the team, and working toward a valuable goal helps team members stay motivated and excited for the work. It also assists them in working together as a team. Petty or interpersonal differences are set aside when everyone is seeking to achieve the same objective.

The team's contributions have value, which must be recognized by the project manager if no one else. Through their daily work, they would contribute to the value of the project. A good PM who acknowledges team member input as valuable can reduce the extras that they may otherwise feel they need to add.

A project manager is also part of the team and should recognize their contributions to value creation. By maintaining a clear vision of what the project is intended to achieve, they can lead the team to success. Staying on the scope and creating the value as mapped out by the client leads to happy clients and satisfied teams.

Thinking Ahead

All projects require a significant amount of planning, even agile projects, in which the project manager expects there will be changes and adjustments throughout the process. With any style of project management, the PM must engage in planning right from the beginning, once they understand entirely what the scope of the project is. There are several different types of skills in this area that a good PM would demonstrate in their work. For most of them, the more projects you can manage, the more you will improve.

- **Time planning** *(aka scheduling)*

    Clients want their project completed by the time that you agreed with upfront. Missing delivery dates makes you a PM that others won't be willing to hire. Being able to estimate how long the various tasks will take is key to agreeing to a doable date.

    If something happens and you realize the date will be missed, you need to be able to communicate such to your client and work toward a new delivery date that you won't miss.

    Early isn't necessarily a positive thing either. Some clients operate on a just-in-time basis, and they won't appreciate having the product taking up space if they can't use it right away. There may be times and projects where the client will appreciate an earlier delivery, but make sure that's the case first if it seems you overestimated the time required.

Lean heavily on your team members with expertise in projects in their domain for solid ideas of each task's timeframe, especially if you haven't done many of these particular projects before. You can also try to find some use cases from similar projects to see what their timeframes looked like.

- **Cost estimation**

As you know, clients hate it when you come back to them with your hand out asking for more money. Get the cost right as *best* you can, and allow yourself some contingency funds *if* you can.

As with time management, it's a good idea to consult with your subject matter experts before bringing a budget to the client if it's a type of work or function that you're not as familiar with.

- **Resource planning**

Knowing how much material and people you will need at the beginning of the project is essential. Rather than continually requesting new items as you go, you can take advantage of the firm's purchasing power in bulk to reduce the cost as much as possible.

People tend to be expensive relative to other resources, so you're better off having enough money in the budget to hire as many people at the outset as you'll need. This is somewhat less of an issue with agile because the team members are cross-functional and can fill in at a variety of tasks. However, in waterfall, you may require some subject matter experts and need to hire people to handle those specific tasks.

Again, it's helpful to consult with others before including any final numbers in the plan you bring to the client. You may have people on your team who can help you make these kinds of estimates, and you can also check the literature to see how similar projects behaved.

- **Critical thinking**

    Successful projects require project managers who can make the right decisions, even under conditions of uncertainty. It's being able to analyze the choices on offer by considering the advantages and disadvantages, along with projecting the likely consequences of each option. Critical thinking allows you to consider the long-term costs and benefits. Then, you can make a confident decision based on the available information, which is usually not all the information you'd like to have before making a choice.

    Although you can consult on possible solutions to a problem, ultimately, you're on your own as far as critical thinking goes. You can't outsource it to more experienced team members or study use cases, although you will get better over time with continual practice.

    One technique that many critical thinkers use is to be contrarian. Being contrarian is considering the opposite viewpoint to the one you currently have and the benefits of that viewpoint. Using this technique can help you broaden your choices and think more creatively about the problem.

- **Strategic thinking**

    As the leader of the project, you're the one who needs to think about the long-term process of the project. Your team members will be focusing on the daily, tactical aspects of it: who does the next piece of work and how. You'll need to manage the daily tasks to ensure they fit in with the long-range vision. Team members have some of the pieces of the puzzle, and you need to make sure they all fit together in a coherent picture.

    You're also the one who must scan the horizon for possible threats and opportunities. For example, a supply chain disruption overseas

could affect the delivery of the resources you've requested. The project manager is responsible for figuring out how to deal with or mitigate the obstacles that inevitably show up during a project.

Like critical thinking, it's a skill that you can't outsource to anyone else. Some barriers to the project are foreseeable, and you can deal with them ahead of time by putting a contingency plan in place. However, some of them will just show up randomly for you to handle.

Being able to listen actively to others' viewpoints will help you improve, as will learning to ask the right questions. That's mostly a matter of practice, as is being able to think through the potential consequences.

One way to practice is to consider not just the first-order consequences (or immediate results), but also about the second order, third order, or results of the results. You can do this for simple decisions in your personal life for practice.

For example, maybe you're considering getting a pet. You know you'll need to prepare your home and pick up bedding, food, and other items. What happens as a result of selecting the bedding? You'll need to find a place for it where the pet will be comfortable. For this example, let's say the only place you can think of is your bedroom. Your new pet might cry at night or make noise because they're not used to their new home. What will you do to mitigate that?

Managing Risk

Have you ever seen a group of meerkats at the zoo or on TV? Most of the animals are scurrying around on the ground, eating, drinking, or hanging out. While they're doing that, there's one that stands up on its hind legs, using its tail for balance, and acting as a lookout. It watches for predators or other threats, which can come by air in the shape of hawks, or on the ground like snakes and jackals.

That's you as a project manager: the lookout meerkat. Your team members are on the ground doing the work and attending to the tasks necessary for project completion. On the other hand, you need to be up on your hind legs and scanning the horizon for threats, no matter where they may come from.

At the beginning of the project, you should be able to list the known risks. Such would provide you with the ability to make contingency plans; so, if the known obstacles emerge, you can shift to your back-up plan or engage the mitigation strategy that you chose. It's important to do this so you can have the budget and resources on hand to deal with problems that you and the team believe are likely to occur.

As with planning skills, you'll improve your risk management as you lead more projects. You can also consult with your team and check the literature for similar projects to see what kinds of risks they faced and how they handled it. This is especially helpful when going into a project, but still, you may not have time to read previous use cases when the unexpected occurs suddenly.

Unlike the lookout meerkat, you're accountable for ensuring that the unexpected wrench in the works doesn't affect your team. If a meerkat threat appears, they will head for their burrows. You need to keep the team working as much as you can; therefore, in addition to mitigating the potential issues known at the start of the project, you'll need to manage the ones you didn't see coming.

You can practice identifying risks or threats, and assigning them probabilities. Some risks have a higher likelihood, but they will have little effect on the project, whereas others may have a lower probability but may stop the project in its tracks. Practice being creative in handling these risks too; you may just find a way to avoid the risk entirely rather than putting your energy into mitigating it.

Be Proactive

As a project manager, you must be a self-starter. You're the one who's large and in charge, and you can't wait for people to tell you what to do and when to do it. You'll often be the person telling others what to do and when! If something isn't working quite the way it should, you have the ultimate responsibility to figure out what's happening and fix it. The bottleneck may be at the client level or in the team. Either way, you'll need to spot it and unclog it so the work can continue.

This is also an indication of maturity. There will be times when you don't feel motivated and you don't want to go to work or tackle a problematic task. However, you still have to do it anyway, without complaint or delay. Project managers must be mature enough to handle roadblocks and a lack of motivation for themselves, not to mention the entire team.

Being proactive is another skill that doesn't lend itself to consulting others. It's a trait that project managers must possess to achieve their objectives. Fortunately, it is something that you can get better at if you're not as self-starting as you'd like to be.

Make sure your focus is on what you can control. If you're constantly worrying about things that you can't influence, you'll start to get frustrated and get burned out pretty quickly. Look only at the issues that you have at least some influence over and let the others go. Practice your prioritization skills, so you ensure that you take care of the issues that affect the project the most first. You won't always know that what you're doing will be successful, but as long as you've thought through the decisions and likely consequences, take action without worrying about the results.

Key Takeaways

A handful of concepts are critical to the success of the project, and you'll need to acquire the associated skills to achieve your goals.

- Scope creep is common and, as a project manager, you need to do everything in your power to avoid it.

- Value creation and commitment are essential for the project and help the team stay on the scope.

- Effective project managers need to master a variety of planning skills.

- They also must be strong risk managers, both for known issues at the outset of the project and of unforeseen obstacles.

- Being proactive is not only a sign of the required maturity but is also necessary for the successful completion of a project.

In the next chapter, you will learn about taking charge of competency and what it really means in the context of project management.

CHAPTER 3

WHAT IS COMPETENCY IN PROJECT MANAGEMENT REALLY ABOUT?

IN an age of specialized skills, many people misunderstand the core competencies for being a leader. Project managers do not need to be experts in every technical task their team completes for the project. They don't necessarily need to be software developers, toy manufacturers, or quality control specialists. It's better for them to have an understanding of these skill sets, but they don't need to master them. The skills that project managers need expertise in are the fundamental skills of a leader.

The Expert Role in Project Management

There are several ways that experts would get involved in the project. Often those who believe themselves to be experts really aren't, which the true experts find greatly annoying! As noted above, the PM isn't expected to be a subject matter expert in the tasks that the team carries out. You definitely want to have team members who've mastered software development when you're working on a software project, but you don't need to be an app master yourself.

Find out what the client is an expert in, which can be helpful on the project. Usually, one area of the client's expertise is in their own company. They've mastered (hopefully) who does what and who can give the necessary permissions to obtain more resources or whatever's at issue. Some clients do know what they're talking about and can be helpful when involved in the project. Others, not so much. When you do have clients who aren't experts trying to be more involved in the project, only to slow things down, it's your responsibility to keep them out of your team's hair so the latter can go about their tasks efficiently. Still, you need to value the client's ideas, even if they're not ideal because they're providing you with a project to manage.

In addition, you need to remember that, even if you're not a master at the underlying task, you are still an expert regarding the project management process. Your client hired you for a reason, and that's to ensure that the project is successful. Even when you're new to the field, you probably know more about project management than the client, so be confident in your communications with them.

Competence as a Leader

You need to be proficient in your project management skills to be seen as competent. Note that I said project management—not functional tasks. As noted earlier in the book, understanding the basics of what your team members are doing is extremely helpful. However, you're not the one who has to be proficient at coding when you're leading a software development team, for example. Those are your functional experts.

The skills in which you need to be proficient are from the strategic perspective, not the daily or weekly tactics. Your competence is measured by your ability to communicate, empower your team, deliver the results, and manage resources and budgets. This is not by how well you code, even if you're a magnificent coder.

Successful PMs need to master these five competencies to be effective at their jobs.

1. Communication

There are a lot of people you need to be able to satisfy when you're the PM, and ensuring that you understand them and they understand you is important. You have your clients, project team members, project sponsor (more detail about them later in the book), and potentially other stakeholders as well.

All these groups are likely to be diverse, with different backgrounds and experiences. On the same project, you may have high school graduates and others with PhDs. The lines of communication must be clear with all of them, no matter what your own experiences and histories are.

With all the people involved in the project, you must be honest and direct without trampling over any relationships or damaging them. When you're able to communicate clearly, you can build more trust, which is a crucial building block to a successful project.

2. Negotiation

Along with all the different stakeholders, there are plenty of competing interests. Your client may want to add what they believe is a small upgrade to the project. Your team members may want to use a specific resource that will help them be more effective at their tasks, but the client's accountant doesn't want to spend the money. You may have competing departments within the client, or you might have battles from your own team between different priorities. Also, you have to manage all these competing interests within the constraints of the budget—picking two of fast, cheap, and good.

In other words, you'll need to be able to negotiate with and between all these interests. An effective PM is always searching for a win-win solution. Not everyone can get everything they want, but, hopefully, you can negotiate so they each get something.

Sometimes, you'll need to compromise. Other times you'll need to maintain a firm line about what can and can't be done on the project in a way that doesn't alienate the people you're saying "no" to.

3. Leadership

Commanding a team and being respected by all the stakeholders in the project are key to the project's success. Rather than using coercion on team members, strong leaders encourage and empower them to achieve the best results they can.

An effective PM can set their own ego aside when dealing with interpersonal relationships. How can they best serve the team and the project? They interact with the various stakeholders without breaking the bonds of trust, even while delivering challenging news.

Everyone can be a leader when they learn to nurture the right capabilities within themselves. You don't have to be an extrovert, just play to your strengths. More details about leadership in project management are coming in the second book of this bundle. But, for now, it's enough to recognize that the more projects you lead and the more time you spend on learning these types of skills, the better off you'll be.

4. Organization and planning skills

As noted in the last chapter, these types of abilities have to be learned through experience and don't depend on the knowledge of others. Many project managers who are more familiar with traditional

project management understand the importance of planning since the entire project must be structured out completely ahead of time before the work even starts.

Yes, these skills are crucial for agile success too. The PM must provide a framework at the beginning of how the project will be completed and plan the iterations as well.

5. Risk management

You learned many of the risk management details in the last chapter. Recall that the important component of risk management is being proactive. This is not waiting to respond until a molehill has become a mountain, but trying to stop an issue at the molehill stage before it can derail the entire project.

You must also recognize where and when you're not the expert. Consult people who've done similar projects when you're embarking on a type of project you haven't completed before. Check in with team members and review the literature if it's available. From time to time, you may discover that one of your stakeholders has some expertise you can tap into, but don't expect that to always be the case.

Vision

As the project manager, you're the one who sees the big picture and how all the smaller pieces fit into it. Stakeholders usually have a more limited view of what's in it for them, and your team members focus on the tactical tasks that they must perform to keep the project on schedule. Not only do you have the vision, but you also need to communicate it to all, then have everyone involved buy into it. All the stakeholders need to understand *how* the project will benefit them and the company, and how your vision will solve their problem.

Once everyone understands the direction and how it will lead to project success, the team can then begin to decide who does what and when. In a waterfall project, the PM leads the way on this task. In agile, with self-organizing teams, the PM may rather consult and encourage to ensure workers use their personal strengths whenever possible.

It's the project manager's job to empower their team to deliver results. That means allowing the team members to figure out the best way to tackle each task. Empowered teams have the maturity to be able to distribute the tasks evenly, the ability to make their own decisions, and the authority and tools to execute.

A team that can't manage its budget for a task and must ask the PM to sign off on the smallest items is not empowered. Such a team may feature pre-assigned roles that don't allow everyone to play to their strengths. They may also be unable to handle their own conflicts, so they must continuously request the project manager to get involved.

Ideally, the project manager is more like a coach once the team starts the project. They're available for consulting and can dive in to help solve a problem. They're managing the big-picture issues, such as potential risks and internal issues with the client, ensuring that all involved on the project are communicating and working together. The whole point of being able to empower the team is so they can handle the functional tasks by themselves once they understand the vision.

That doesn't mean they have free rein over the entire project, however. Teams need boundaries. For example, purchasing items under $100 may not require approval from the PM, but those over the threshold do. If the team wants to include an upgrade that will delay the timeline of the project, they should get the project manager's approval. However, daily decisions and relationship issues would be handled among themselves.

When a project manager doesn't give their team the power to make these decisions, it causes problems for everyone. The timeline will be

slowed down because the members have to wait for the PM to approve every decision, no matter how minute. Rather than attempting to solve problems on their own, whether interpersonal or having to do with the task itself, the team members have no incentive to try to hash it out themselves. Instead, they'll depend on the PM to get them through the smallest ordeal. Because they're not trying to solve anything themselves, creativity will drop as well, since the only solution is the one the PM comes up with.

We've talked about how much more satisfied workers are at their jobs when they have some control over their day. A team that doesn't have the power to execute the project manager's vision doesn't have control over their tasks and schedules, so their productivity and job satisfaction drop as well. Being able to empower the team will make a huge difference to the success or failure of the project.

Leading with vision requires a dedication to continuous learning. Keeping up with technology and changing times is key to being able to execute that vision by having the appropriate tools ready for the team. If, at any point, you as a project manager can find something new that will help your team perform the work faster, more efficiently, and more easily, the better off everyone is.

It also requires some smart risk-taking on your part. Be bold when you're looking for breakthroughs. Playing it safe means fewer opportunities to excel. Taking intelligent chances is the only way to innovate. You'll need to game out the possible consequences of these actions first, which is the smart way to go about it. Maybe you'll need to consult with others who have been in similar situations, and perhaps you need to take your team's temperature first. However, don't ignore solutions or improvements just because they're not guaranteed to work. Think about them and the first-order consequences, then the second and third before you make a decision. Don't spend too much time in analysis paralysis, but go for it when the odds are with you.

Key Takeaways

Competency for project managers is measured in their ability to manage the entire project, not just accomplish certain functional tasks.

- You are the expert in project management, whereas your team members are subject matter experts on their tasks.

- Competent project managers are proficient in putting the pieces of the project puzzle together into a cohesive whole, and managing the relationships around it.

- Setting the vision, then empowering the team to deliver it is the most efficient way for a PM to work with their team.

In the next chapter, you will learn how to use the client's management to your advantage as a project manager.

CHAPTER 4

OUTSIDE THE PETRI DISH: MANAGEMENT CULTURE AND ORGANIZATIONAL BEHAVIOR

IT might seem obvious that the organization you're working with on a project would do anything in its power to make the project successful. As the project manager, you've set a clear vision for the project and how it benefits all the stakeholders, and you have benchmarks for success. Why wouldn't management be wholly captivated and willing to support you?

Unfortunately, you'll run into situations where it doesn't seem like management has your back. In fact, from time to time, you might find yourself under the wheels of the proverbial bus when they try to blame you for project failure! The more buy-in you get from management, especially the upper parts of the hierarchy, the more support you'll have throughout the project.

"Project management methodologies, regardless how good, are simply pieces of paper. What converts these pieces of paper into a world-class methodology is the culture of the organization and how quickly project management is accepted and used. Superior project management is attained when the organization has a culture based on effective trust, communication, cooperation, and teamwork." — Harold Kerzner, well-known management consultant and author

If only the PM's job were as simple as managing the Triple Constraint triangle! The project manager is the one who needs to build trust between the project team and the organization, so the team can receive the resources it needs for a successful project without too much interference from other stakeholders. When the team isn't supported, the PM will struggle to communicate, obtain the required resources, and encourage the team through the obstacles.

The most significant factor in project success is the organizational culture (Machado dos Santos et al., 2019).[6] The next most important is change management, which we'll discuss in a later chapter, and support from top management.

Organizational Culture

Also known as corporate culture, this is the beliefs, attitudes, behaviors, and values of the company's employees. Components of organizational culture include:

- Perspective on authority and leadership
- Shared vision and expectations
- Work ethic
- Social norms
- Incentive systems
- Code of conduct
- Risk management

For successful and mature organizations, project management culture is integral to the way they strategize and operate their business. It's embedded in the workplace, including the reward and motivation systems, and how the rank and file view leadership. A culture that recognizes and embraces project management is one that boosts the potential success rate of its projects. Its senior management comprehends the value of project management, aligns projects with business objectives, and demonstrates their commitment to their projects by investing time and money into them.

Senior managers in a strong project management culture demonstrate the type of leadership they want to see in all levels of the hierarchy. When they spot roadblocks in the way of a project, they come in and remove the barriers. Projects aren't an activity that's occasionally done outside the business plan or strategic objectives; they're an integral part of the daily work that occurs at the company, and their successes and failures are taken as seriously by the executives as any other business initiative.

A company's culture is its DNA, which shapes the behavior of its workers. Unfortunately, it's more fragile than human DNA because a mature project management culture can be destroyed with leadership that doesn't value or understand project management. Top executives forge the path for successful culture and can just as easily destroy it when they don't visibly support the projects and project teams at work.

As a project manager, when you're working for a solid project management culture, you'll know it because leadership has identified the responsibilities of your role and supports you in your work. Unfortunately, not all companies have a strong project management culture. Some may have weak cultures where project management isn't considered a key aspect of the business. However, with some prodding and building the case for project management, this type of organization can become one with strong project support.

More difficult are the firms where the company culture is strong, but project management is immature. These types of companies concentrate on functional tasks rather than cross-functional projects and don't understand the value that projects bring to the business. They may be harder to transform into a strong and mature organization because you'll be fighting the entrenched culture to make changes.

The overall project success rate in an organization reflects both its culture and the maturity of its project management function.

Values of the Project Management Culture

When the right values that support project management are embodied in the organization, there's a huge difference in how employees behave.

- **Communication**

    When this value is present, workers have an open dialogue with each other and with their superiors. Management has an open-door policy, which will also lead to more cooperation. Communication and cooperation feed off each other in a mature firm. Discussions are held regularly, both within levels of the hierarchy and between them, and employees understand what management is thinking and vice versa. Status reports are quick and short because everyone knows what's going on.

    When there isn't much communication, there aren't many people whom employees can talk to openly. Instead of short reports, there must be formal (and long) status meetings to catch everyone up to the latest data. All communication must be documented, which takes enormous amounts of time.

- **Trust**

    Employees who trust leadership and each other, and organizations that trust project management, are successful in their work. All levels of management are project sponsors (discussed in detail in the next chapter), and KPIs are aligned with the projects.

    When there is no trust, there's also very little success, competition among employees and management, less work completed, and more power grabs. KPIs are misaligned with projects.

- **Teamwork**

    Everyone feels free to share when there's a healthy attitude promoting teamwork in the business. Employees are committed to their own work, but also that of the team, and they leverage each other's strengths.

    Good luck getting projects completed when teamwork is not a core value! If anything gets shared, it's only for the employee's glory. There are no personal bonds between the workers or management; thus no one is committed to the team.

- **Cooperation**

    Here, you have support up and down the management hierarchy. Strategies include project management, and they are clearly communicated. Goals are also coherent and explicit.

    How does it look when there is no cooperation or support? "It's not my job" to ensure project success, so no one ends up doing the job. Not only are priorities not aligned with the projects, but there may be sabotage that tries to ensure the project does not succeed.

Conditions for Active Management Support

Given that top management's support is one of the critical factors in project success, you can see that it's necessary to get buy-in from the highest levels of leadership. Those lower on the ladder take their cues from their superiors. If the CEO can't be bothered and doesn't seem to think the project is important, so why should anyone else? Once the top of the pyramid is actively supporting the project, the lower levels will follow.

It's not enough for managers to say that they're only responsible for the project being behind schedule. They also need to demonstrate their interest. Ask the team what they can do to help, and, if there is anything, deliver on it. Employees are quick to notice when their management is all talk and no action. Project success depends on active support from all levels of the hierarchy.

Management must stand behind the team, whether they're progressing or not. No fair-weather support will make a project successful! Only 100% backing will allow the PM to complete it on time and budget.

Driving Active Support

The best way to ensure that project management is successful within an organization is to bake it into the company's business plan, vision, and mission. When integrated properly, projects align with the values and financials of the firm, where project success means company success. When senior executives have the incentive to support project managers proactively, there's little work on the PM's part to get their buy-in. The project manager, in this case, feels that progress is made easily and they can rely on the executives for the support they need.

Once an organization embraces project management into its cultural values, it can then set up a framework that helps them initiate the

right projects and deliver them successfully. There are three levels of management: those at the senior executive level, senior management, and line management.

Senior executives working within such a culture demonstrate their commitment regularly to project management in a variety of ways.

- **Align projects with business objectives**

    The more people have an incentive to support a project, the easier it will be to get buy-in! When it's clear how the project will support the business, everyone has a reason to support it.

    When the project isn't aligned clearly with the business plan, it becomes easier for management to downplay the project as optional, or as something that's "nice to have." When it's necessary to achieve the goals of the firm, no manager or executive will want to downplay it or stand in the way of its success.

- **Implement organizational and portfolio project management**

    Organizational project management is what the organization uses to align project (along with program and portfolio) management with its strategy and objectives, and customize practices to fit within the culture and structure of the firm.

    A program consists of a group of related projects. Portfolio project management groups piece together all the projects and programs to create one single place for oversight and management of them, and adopt standardized governance across the organization.

    Putting both these frameworks in place is a way for the organization to embed the principles of project management into its practices. It ensures that all projects across the organization operate under the same standards and are governed in the same way.

- **Educated in project management and its benefits**

    When senior executives understand how beneficial project management can be for their KPIs, it becomes much easier for them to support projects actively. They are familiar with how the process works and when and how they can best provide feedback when appropriate. They're aware that obstacles and issues arise during the execution of the project and do their best to mitigate them so that the team can continue with their work uninterrupted. In addition, they understand the necessity for them to be visible to the project teams and others, so everyone in the organization knows they're providing support.

- **Development and career growth**

    For project teams to work at their best, they must always be in the process of continuous learning. Providing training and development is a key method to demonstrate that the organization supports project management because they're investing money and time into it.

    This type of human resource development also includes developing project managers and furthering their careers. Investing in PMs is a clear signal that the organization values them.

- **Establish project management culture**

    Traditional company culture is sometimes at odds with project management, particularly when it's agile. Project teams value communication and feedback during the process—not just at the final delivery. Operating in short sprints and iterations may be uncomfortable for those who are more used to a traditional form of work.

    Project management culture embraces these differences and encourages more feedback, not just within teams, but also with other departments and sections. Having a view of all the

stakeholders involved in an issue is a project management staple that can also be extremely helpful in management, yet not everyone embraces it.

Senior management has its role to play in successful project management as well.

- **Recognize positive ROI and achieve KPIs**

    If you don't recognize this alphabet soup, that's OK! ROI is an acronym for Return On Investment. Senior managers who seek higher ROI from projects are more willing to take on other projects and support the project teams.

    KPI stands for Key Performance Indicator, which is management-speak for the metrics that senior management is often responsible for. Successful projects can improve performance, so smart senior managers will do their best to support a project's successful completion.

- **Remove barriers to project success**

    The project manager can't do everything themselves. Sometimes, there are barriers within the organization that may otherwise prevent the project's success. Senior managers who are steeped in the project management culture and know how much successful completion can boost their metrics will remove roadblocks that could get in the way.

- **Provide necessary resources**

    Project teams need more resources than just their brainpower. They may need materials, expert team members, or even just the opportunity to get their questions answered by an expert on the organization. Senior management is well placed to give them what they need.

- **Establish guidelines and strategy**

    These are particularly important when multiple projects are going on at the same time. Projects should be executed in a reasonable timeframe that matches up with the company's business objectives. They may be unable to devote enough resources to too many projects at once, so they need to be prioritized.

    The firm may also want to establish guidelines around what dollar (or time) amounts require management approval before changes can be made, what the PMs are and aren't responsible for, etc.

    Senior management, with their overview of the entire company, can put these in place effectively, so all the projects can operate smoothly and similarly to each other.

Finally, **line management** is also key to the project's success.

- **Provide skilled resources**

    The project team may need an expert from the organization to help them out or answer their questions, and line managers are the ones who can approve the worker shifting their time to the project. Managers who see that their superiors support the project and who have their incentives aligned with the project can then juggle the need for resources efficiently.

- **Ensure commitments are met**

    Line management is responsible for ensuring that the experts are provided, along with other resources where appropriate. When they're committed to the project's success, PMs find they have all the resources possible.

If you, as a PM, encounter an organization that demonstrates most or all of the above criteria at every level of management, consider yourself lucky. You're working with a firm that values project management

and will support you and your team in delivering a successful project. This is a mature company (in terms of projects anyway) that understands and already values project managers.

Gaining Management Support

Unfortunately, you might not be working with a mature firm. You may end up working with companies that don't provide this type of support, yet you still need the buy-in of management. How do you go about securing support from an organization that isn't already set up to do it?

If a project has been authorized and a budget allocated to it, then someone bought into the idea. Likely, it was someone in the upper levels of management because lower-level types typically don't have the authorization for it. However, once the executives signed off on the agreement, they may not educate the rest of management on why the project is important and why it should be supported. That part is now up to you. If you can find and develop a project sponsor (which we'll discuss more in the next chapter), that will be a great advantage.

On the other hand, what if you can't find a project sponsor and you're dealing with a less mature firm? You may need to do a little digging, and whoever authorized the project (or their assistant) will be the best place to start when figuring out what you need to know.

"Show me the incentive and I'll show you the outcome."
—Charlie Munger

1. Who are the stakeholders, and where are they in the company hierarchy?

Your team needs to understand who your project will affect and how the change affects them. Each stakeholder group likely has at least a manager or supervisor, and they may also have a person of influence who can help you reach buy-in with the group.

You also need to understand where they are in the hierarchy because, if the supervisor of one of the groups won't take a step without their manager's approval, you will need to know that so you can approach their manager first.

Suppose you've been hired by the Chief Communications Officer (CCO) of a company to develop a marketing dashboard for the communications analysts. Obviously, the communications analysts are a stakeholder group representing users of the dashboard. They may or may not report to the same manager because they could be in different functional areas or business units. You will need buy-in from their managers.

Who do the managers report to? With a flat structure for the organization, they could all report to the Senior Vice-President of marketing, who would report directly to the CCO. You'd also need buy-in from the senior VP; however, with more complex organizations, there may be an intermediate layer of management between the Senior VP and the CCO, both of whom need to be involved. Otherwise, the managers may not all report to the same VP, so you would need to add them in.

Are you finished with stakeholders? Maybe not. Who else uses the data from the marketing dashboard? Perhaps the communications analysts send out reports and the new dashboard changes to the creative team. You'll need to get buy-in from their manager too.

In other words, there are probably multiple levels of managers and stakeholder groups that you'll need to work with to increase your project's probability of success. Do your best to identify them and see where they fall on the org chart.

2. What are their metrics

This might be a little more difficult to dig up, but you can probably make some educated guesses if you can't get the hard data on how the various managers and workers are incentivized.

For example, the communications analysts may have targets for the number of pieces they complete during the week, and the manager's KPI is based on that. Senior VPs may have incentives tied to the budget, ROI, or a number of leads generated by a piece of marketing material, among other things.

If you know what their metrics are and what they get rewarded for, you'll know how to tailor your message to them. This way, you can increase the value for the stakeholders because it fits their KPIs and, as a result, they will be more than willing to support you.

3. Tune into station WII-FM

Take a step back and imagine that you're in the shoes of one of your stakeholders. They haven't been told why they should support this project, but have had it foisted upon them, at least in their minds. If you're leading an external team, they won't know you nor do they have any reason to trust you. Depending on the size of the company, they may have never met the person who signed off on their project.

They may not like what they're currently doing (that you're coming in to change), and they might have complained about it for some time, but it's familiar to them. There's a reason why people stay in their ruts, even when they're not particularly happy with them; change is unknown and, therefore, scary. These stakeholders know how to deal with whatever the current issues are, and now they've been told they have to take on new issues. If you were in that position, would you be happy about it?

If you've ever been in marketing, you may have recognized station WII-FM. It's an easy acronym to remember what you need to think about from the perspective of your stakeholder groups:

What's In It For Me?

Why should they accept this change that the senior executive has decreed for them? Because it makes their lives better in some way.

Making it faster, easier, and more efficient, it automates the boring, menial stuff so that they can get on with the more exciting parts of the job. It provides a higher ROI, doubles the lead generation from a single piece of marketing content ("collateral"), and gets rid of the bottleneck. Hence, the process takes much less time, and gathers all the data in one place so clients don't have to root through six different systems to analyze results.

For each stakeholder group, you need to explain *clearly* what's in it for them. It's not about the features of whatever you're putting in place, but how it improves their lives. For example, who wants a marketing dashboard? The CCO, but who else? Otherwise, people may wish to an easy-to-use system in which they can see how a single piece of collateral performed across all social media platforms.

They might want a system that tracks their ad dollars spent online with the number of prospects who clicked on the ad link. This is known as CPC or cost per click. Being able to track CPC across all platforms at once makes it easy to see where the company should be spending its ad dollars, rather than wasting people's time adding up numbers in a spreadsheet. Automating menial tasks so your analysts can do more powerful work is something people buy into.

This may not apply to the Senior VP, who likely doesn't care if the users are totting up numbers in a spreadsheet or using software. However, this one marketing dashboard means the six other pieces of software being used to deliver data to the spreadsheets are no longer necessary and can be reduced, saving huge amounts of time and expenses. There's an incentive for anyone with budget authority.

Once you can identify the people who need to demonstrate their support for the project victory, you can then make your case to them. Think in terms of **"head, heart, and hands"** (May, 2016).[7]

- **Communicate**

    It should be just like voting: early and often. It should also be taken seriously; however, make sure you and team members are regularly in touch while continuing to feed the reasons for what's in it for the stakeholders, which helps them understand why they should support the team.

    It also sends the message that the project team values the stakeholders' input and concerns, which gives the latter a feeling of control and validation, making them more likely to support you.

- **Build the business case**

    Many managers, especially those with authority over their resources, need to see how the project supports their departments and goals. If they see how it will increase ROI, improve their KPIs, or help them retain more clients and increase client satisfaction, they will then have a good reason to support the project.

    Do your best to build a case that supports all the stakeholder groups. Then, you just have one document that you can bring to meetings with all the different departments in play.

- **Document how the managers can help you in specific action items**

    You can sometimes win over the managers, but they may not be sure how they can demonstrate their support. Maybe you identified interdepartmental meetings where the manager can express their backing of the project and how they've devoted time or resources to it.

    The more specific actions you can find, the better. People in management tend to be action-oriented; thus they feel better when they know what they can do to bring about the desired outcome—in your case, a successful project.

- **Measure progress with buy-in**

    As the project's work commences, check in with your stakeholders to measure how much they're supporting and want to support the project. Once you've convinced them of how they'll benefit specifically from the work, they will believe that it's how they can achieve their goals. At that stage, you have their hearts. Once they join you in the work, even if just to provide you with the resources you need, you have their hands.

    You also want to watch for stakeholders who *aren't* buying into the project. What are their remaining concerns? Was communication with them not persuasive?

If you're having difficulty with getting buy-in, even after you've done this work, ask yourself (and management) why. Do they think the project will shift their strategy or culture in ways they're concerned about? Are there financial issues on the horizon? Management may or may not be willing to share, but this is helpful information for you to know.

Organizational Change Management (OCM)

This is the approach companies use when they want or need to change their culture, such as moving from an inefficient or ambivalent project management organization to a mature one. A project manager leads many of these programs, but they require additional skills compared to a standard project that's not about changing the firm's identity.

As you've probably experienced in your own business and personal lives, human beings are very resistant to change. It turns out there's a neurological basis for it, making it potentially hardwired in (Gilbert, 2012).[8]

Essentially, the brain detects a change in the environment. That signal goes to the prefrontal cortex, which is where reasoning and

higher functioning reside. This part of the brain compares that change with what's stored already in the mind and existing habits (basal ganglia). If those two don't match up, an error signal is then sent to the amygdala.

The amygdala is the area of the brain that was inherited from our reptilian ancestors and contains the fight-or-flight reflex, among other quick reactions and reflexes intended to get our ancestors out of danger. In other words, the amygdala can't tell whether it's fighting a sabertoothed cat or merely an information error; it only knows that the brain is under attack. So, it amps up the fear reaction, including stress hormones like cortisol, increases the breathing rate (so you can take in more oxygen as you're running away from predators), among other reactions.

This is the main reason why people resist change. Their brains think they're being chased across the country by a predator, which adds a degree of difficulty to the process! Unfortunately, it's not an appropriate reaction to change in the workplace, and trying to tell the amygdala that will yield poor results. However, that's what you're dealing with when you're leading and organizing OCM.

Many different frameworks for successful change management have been used in large and small businesses. Ultimately, OCM is taking the firm from its current state to its future state. When dealing with a culture that doesn't understand the value of project management right now, you're taking it from being ambivalent about projects or strongly immature to an organization that fully supports project management and is invested in the success of its projects at all levels of management.

1. Prep the organization for change

Here's where your vision as a project manager can be used to full effect. To convince the firm that they need to buy into project management, you must show them what kind of wonderful world awaits them on the other side.

What are the benefits of the strong culture that incorporates projects into their business plans and objectives? How does it make their lives easier or work more efficient and productive? Most importantly, you should think about how well-managed projects can ensure strategic goals are achieved.

Create that tension between what they have now, what is sub-optimal, and the future state. They need to understand that there is a gap before they can decide to change it.

You'll need to get buy-in from senior leadership at the beginning, which you'll then use to build at the lower levels of the hierarchy as well. Share the vision, so they can clearly recognize what they're missing by not building this culture. Then, develop the plan to bridge that gap. They'll see what's not working while also realizing they can have an improved future. With your help, they can get *there* from *here*.

You'll need to draw on your communications skills at this stage and throughout the project. Showing them that gap consistently and letting them know how they will cross it will help them internalize how change can and should be done.

2. Make adjustments to the operations

This is the most difficult stage because it requires you to fight that neurological resistance to change. It can be done, and putting yourself in the employees' shoes to comprehend what you're asking them to do is a crucial part of getting this step right. When you understand their fears, you'll know how to combat them effectively.

In this stage, managers must model the behaviors they want to see, which will help the firm bridge the gap. They'll need to clarify what's acceptable and what isn't. This needs to happen with your help

because *you* are the expert in project management, and you can tell them what's effective in a strong culture.

Most importantly, the business structures and incentives must be aligned with project management success for change to benefit the company. Projects must become part of the business planning and be considered in the business objectives. Managers and supervisors also need to be rewarded for project success, so they can have more reasons to support the projects.

All while this is happening, you, as a PM, need to remind everyone of the vision regularly. This will include why they're being asked to overcome their natural resistance to change and do things differently. Change is hard, and all must have the vision consistently in their minds, so they can execute the tasks necessary to achieve it.

Workers should be empowered to decide how to make the required adjustments wherever possible. If they see roadblocks, they can devise a new method to overcome them. The more choice and control they have over their work, the less resistance to change that the management team will face.

3. Make sure it sticks

At this stage, the leaders need to "refreeze" the new habits and behaviors to ensure the new project management culture becomes entrenched firmly. They need to prevent backsliding when it (almost inevitably) occurs and make sure the changes are institutionalized in the culture, documentation, and procedures.

From time to time, they should review their progress to ensure the change is occurring on schedule and so they can spot any backsliding that may happen.

BEING AN EFFECTIVE PROJECT MANAGER | CHAPTER 4

Key Takeaways

Having an organization that buys into project management at all levels of the management hierarchy is a major factor in the success of your projects. If that type of mature culture doesn't exist, you may need to lead organizational change or, at the very least, build management support for the project.

- Mature organizational culture prizes and supports project management.

- Immature cultures need change management to increase their buy-in for projects and become mature.

- The support of management is key at all levels—from senior executives down to line management.

- If you don't have this support, you can build it using different strategies with different management positions.

In the next chapter, you will learn how to use project sponsorship to help you win.

---

[6] https://**doi.org**/10.1590/0103-6513.20180108
[7] https://**www.dashe.com**/blog/the-importance-of-stakeholder-buy-in
[8] https://**www.batimes.com**/articles/the-change-management-life-cycle-involve-your-people-to-ensure-success.html

CHAPTER 5

PROJECT SPONSORS: THE KEYS TO THE PROJECT MANAGEMENT KINGDOM

HAVING a good project sponsor can make or break a project. As a project manager, it's up to you to cultivate these relationships to make your life (and that of the project team) so much easier. If you work for an immature organization, there may be no project sponsor, or the one who is present may cause more problems than they solve. There are ways to help sponsors become more effective and also some methods that can help you neutralize those that could be working against you.

Who Is a Project Sponsor?

This person "owns" the project, has the highest interest in it, and is responsible for providing resources and support to the project. Ideally, they would smooth the way for the project team to be successful, helping senior management buy into the project, and removing any barriers that stand in the way. They typically initiate the project and get involved from day one. Normally, they're the ones who select the PM.

They are the champion of the project within the organization. They achieve buy-in from management, ensure that the lower-level managers are on board with the project, and provide the necessary resources. There are three primary obligations for the project sponsor: governance, vision, and value (Malsam, 2019).[9]

1. Governance

- Initiates the project
- Defines roles and responsibilities
- Supports the project's organization
- Provides resources
- Escalates for issues the PM can't handle themselves

2. Vision

- Aligns business case with business objectives, strategy, and plan
- Defines the success of the project and how it fits into the business strategy

3. Value

- Manages risks
- Controls and reviews the process
- Assists with decision making
- Determines project quality
- Assesses progress
- Ensures the project delivers value with positive results

You can see there's some overlap between the project manager and project sponsor duties, but the sponsor is the one who is ultimately accountable for the success of the project.

Collaboration Between the Project Manager and Sponsor

Since the sponsor is the one who can make the PM's life either easy or difficult, the project manager must cooperate with the sponsor as best they can. The sponsor provides the environment in which the PM can either sink or swim, can muster the resources that the project manager needs, and takes care of internal issues that the PM cannot resolve.

It's also the sponsor's charge to ensure that the project team, including the manager, understands how their project will impact the business. They must know how the business case aligns with the objectives and strategies of the firm as a whole. Then, they will have a sense of pride in their work because it's a crucial component of the company's success. The project becomes meaningful in a way it otherwise may not have been.

Unlike project or risk management, there aren't any codified frameworks for steps the project manager should take to work with the sponsor. However, there are known activities that can increase the probability of a successful working relationship.

- **Meet early and often**

    Developing a good partnership right away will help both people in their quest for project success. The PM needs to update the sponsor regularly on how the project is progressing, along with any potential risks they see coming over the horizon. As the sponsor should be well-respected in their firm and be able to communicate well with other members of the management team, they can use this prior knowledge to prevent issues from overwhelming the project.

The more they meet, the more trust they will build in each other, which is a critical factor in success. Even though both may have busy schedules while the project is ongoing, continuing to touch base periodically must be part of the schedule.

- **Define rules of engagement**

    The sponsor and manager need to work together to understand how the project will fit into the business. This includes how they will work with each other and how the project team will cooperate with the sponsor and other employees of the firm. In this way, nothing will be omitted or left out of the planning because both clearly understand the structure of the engagement.

- **Discuss the roles and expectations**

    What is the PM responsible for? Likewise, what is the sponsor? These guidelines should also be laid out at the beginning. Nothing gets overlooked, and there are fewer problems later on.

    Just as the PM takes on the tactical aspects of the project and allows team members to focus on daily tasks, so too does the effective sponsor avoid getting bogged down in the project details.

    Once the guidelines for the engagement and trust in the team have been established, the sponsor does not necessarily need to be hands-on with the project. They understand that the PM will keep them updated on progress and escalate anything the PM can't handle, or that would be more appropriate coming from the sponsor.

There are several actions that the PM should expect from a **good sponsor**:

- Design a robust project charter with the project manager.
- Participate meaningfully during the kickoff meetings.
- Approve only frameworks and plans that seem feasible in terms of time, money, and resources.
- Evaluate project progress against benchmarks and guide the PM.
- Prevent scope creep.
- Celebrate reaching key project milestones with the team.
- Remove roadblocks where possible.
- Participate in after-project assessments and evaluations.
- Ensure successful hand-offs, so changes aren't dropped after completion.
- Sign off on the completed project.

The PM's ability and the complexity of the project should dictate the level of support from the sponsor. When the project manager is new to the type of project they're managing or the complexity is higher, the sponsor should be more involved. If it's not too complex, the PM may need more coaching. However, if it's higher, the sponsor needs to be more hands-on and involved directly, yet still maintaining the more strategic approach.

When the project isn't as intricate and the PM is experienced, the sponsor should be mostly hands-off and can rely on the project manager for updates. For more complicated projects, the sponsor should support the PM more and act as a consultant.

Most questions that the PM needs to ask the sponsor should appear early in the engagement, so the division of roles and priorities are clear. They need to ensure the sponsor will provide necessary resources, and that they understand their obligations.

Problem Sponsors, Problem Projects

In an organization with a strong project management culture, where everyone from line managers to top executives understands the benefits and why the project is necessary, you probably won't have many problems, if any, with your sponsor. The firm will have sponsors who are knowledgeable about project benefits, can articulate them and encourage buy-in among the other levels of management, understand how to work with PMs, and provide them with the environment they need to complete a successful project. These sponsors are vocal and visible with their support and will try to remove any impediments to project success. They want you, as a PM, to communicate with them regularly, avoid "shooting the messenger," and empower you and your team to get the work done.

Unfortunately, you will run into sponsors who... are pretty much the exact opposite of that. Typically, you'll see them in immature organizations. Sometimes they're just clueless, though often they will attempt to micromanage the project instead of empowering you to deliver the goods. If they can't empower you to do your job, either they picked the wrong PM, or the organization selected the wrong sponsor. In some cases, it's both.

They're like seagulls, and you want to avoid them whenever possible. According to Kenneth Blanchard, "Seagull managers fly in, make a lot of noise, dump on everyone, then fly out" (1985)[10]. They try to manage all the details of the project, despite how that's not their job. Since they're not the experts in project management, and you are, this could result in disaster.

If you have a seagull sponsor, you can look forward to a difficult life as a project manager because they'll engage in some or all of the following behaviors:

- Constant questioning or even ignoring your decisions as a PM.
- Micromanages the project.
- Doesn't understand the benefits of project management or the specific project you're managing.
- Discourages you from raising negative issues.
- Takes credit for successes, but blames you for failures.
- Changes priorities on a whim.
- Asks for long and detailed status reports frequently.

Build a Better Sponsor

If you see red flags waving when you first meet your project sponsor, and you're concerned you have a seagull, fortunately, there are some concrete steps you can take to try to develop them into a sponsor who will help you instead of hinder you.

Do a little research on them before you get started. LinkedIn is a great place to start looking because many professionals use this platform to network. Just be aware that if the sponsor has the Sales Navigator application, they can see the names of people who have viewed their profile.

See if you can find any commonalities: anything in your background that matches theirs. Even attending the same college, whether you did so at the same time, is a great starting point. Otherwise, you can see if they're engaged in any similar groups. This can help you build a connection with them, along with some trust, right away. This works with good project sponsors too.

Sit down with them to discuss the roles and responsibilities. You may find the use of a checklist helpful to ensure that you hit all the main points. Document the meeting and make sure the sponsor has a record of what you both agreed to.

You'll need to spend some time with the sponsor to help them understand what their role is and why it is important, along with why the project is necessary. If you had to develop a business case for senior management, you'd also find it helpful here. There are five methods you can use to influence them to become a better sponsor.

1. Communicate, communicate, communicate

To build trust, you may need to be in touch with them more often than you want or think you have time for. However, they need to see that you aren't trying to hide sensitive issues and that you're timely with potential issues as well—not delaying anything. This communication also includes regular update meetings.

2. Stay tuned to WII-FM

Here's where your research and business case really pay off. You should have a sense of your sponsor's incentives and interests, so you can appeal to what they care about. How does the successful completion of the project benefit your sponsor specifically? Not just the company as a whole, but *for them*? Continue to remind them of what's in it for them throughout the project—not only in the beginning.

3. Appeal to their desire to be a great sponsor

Most people enjoy mastering their position. They want to be good at it and have others view them as professionals. Let this innate desire help you work with them. Let them know how successful sponsors act and communicate. As always, tie it back to what's in it for them; how will being recognized as a good sponsor benefit them and their career?

4. Continue to focus on the common goal: a successfully completed project

Ultimately, the project is not about you as a project manager or them as a project sponsor. It's about the completion of a project that

achieves its goals and objectives. As they say in 12-step programs: "Principles before personalities."

5. Avoid being condescending or using the word "should"

You're indeed the expert in project management, but you can still derail a relationship by acting as if you know everything and the other person knows nothing. Treat them as equals—remember that, likewise, there's a lot they know that you don't!

Do you enjoy it when other people tell you that you *should* do this, or *should not* do that? If you don't enjoy it, make sure you don't use such language with your sponsor either. Value and build a bridge with them; don't tear it down.

One method to get your point across without too much "should-ing" is to tell them stories of what you've seen work for you and others, and what hasn't worked in similar situations. Most people like stories and they can connect those dots pretty quickly. They won't feel like you're trying to decide for them or that they're giving up control, which everyone hates. In this case, you're not telling them what to do, but giving them options.

Keep them involved in the project as well. If you ask for their input on some higher-level decisions or to help brainstorm, they'll see that you respect them and their work. That helps them trust you while giving them more of a feeling of control.

Obviously, you would rather have a solid sponsor from the get-go; one who works in a mature organization and is developed enough to handle the responsibility of being the owner of the project. However, it doesn't always happen that way. It's up to you, as a project manager, to make sure you have the best sponsor you can, even if they didn't want or don't know how to do the job. Your maturity, as a PM, will be of great benefit when working with a sub-optimal sponsor because you'll need to take the lead in building the connection and developing the trust between you.

Key Takeaways

The project sponsor is the owner of the project and can champion a project to its success or completely derail it. As a project manager, when you run into a weak sponsor, you'll need to take over some of those responsibilities while you build them into a better one.

- The project sponsor is a critical factor in the project's success, and a good one will empower you and the team while removing roadblocks to success.

- As a PM, you should meet with the sponsor early to decide the rules of engagement and determine the structure of who does what.

- A good project sponsor does not micromanage the PM and adjusts their level of support according to the project manager's experience and the complexity of the project.

- Bad project sponsors may get bogged down in the details of the project and override the PM's decisions.

- If you end up with a weak sponsor, there are ways that you can work with them to build a better connection and develop them into the kind of sponsor that helps you rather than blocks you.

In the next chapter, you will learn how to close a project for success.

---

9 https://www.projectmanager.com/blog/what-is-a-project-sponsor
10 https://en.wikipedia.org/wiki/Seagull_management

CHAPTER 6

ALWAYS BE CLOSING

THE end of the project is just delivering the results that were defined in the scope, right? Not exactly. For the project to be completed successfully, there is a hand-off at the end. In addition, project managers need to deliver *throughout* the entire project process—not just at the end. There are many steps along the way that result in a thriving project, and too many wrong actions jeopardize that success just as an immature project management culture can.

Strong Execution

As a project manager, your job isn't over after you've planned everything out, at the beginning of the project, or after the sprint. Your job is to balance the supervision of the whole process and get involved where necessary while preventing yourself from being bogged down in the details or not empowering your team, so they must come to you for every small decision. Effective PMs do get their hands dirty, often with supervisory tasks like ensuring that someone follows up on the action items, adding needed resources, and the all-important skill of herding cats.

You have to stay on top of the project and make sure that deadlines are met. Since you may be the only one who can see how the puzzle fits together, you have to be in constant communication with the other pieces to make sure any issues are being handled appropriately or escalated to you when necessary. It's easy for team members to focus only on the task in front of them, so they need you to keep the big picture in view and help them align their work with the objectives of the process.

Just as the project sponsor is responsible for removing barriers to the project's completion and ensuring that management isn't interfering with the process, you need to do the same for your project team. They should be able to focus on the work while you handle external risks and barriers.

At the same time, you're working with people, so they must all feel comfortable coming to you with problems or issues that arise. That includes both stakeholders and members of your team. Having empathy and being able to listen actively are two key traits for an effective PM. If you ask your team where they're getting stuck and pay attention to the answer, it will be much easier to tackle roadblocks on their behalf.

Also, help your team look good in front of the stakeholders by supporting them in preparing presentations or other materials for meetings. It's not your job to create the designs or make the copies, but ensure there are no mistakes and everything hangs together coherently. Not everyone is skilled verbally, so they may need more assistance in putting the documents together. Your task

is also to massage the tone of the message and level of details according to the needs of the stakeholders they will meet.

As a PM, you're also the head prioritizer for the project once the sponsor and stakeholders have agreed on the scope. You probably won't be able to deal with everything at once, so your job is to prioritize the top three or four tasks or goals that are most important to the project's success at any given time, and guide the team accordingly.

You'll likely have a lot of information coming your way, some of which is helpful, whereas some not as much. In other words, you'll be taking on the role of a filter as well. If the info assists the team, you can let it through; otherwise, scrap or archive it if you think you may need it later. This allows the team to focus on the work without too many outside distractions because you will take care of it.

Stress is something that many PMs experience, particularly with all the distractions they're faced with. To prepare for stress, make sure that you have time to exercise, provide yourself with a pleasant night-time environment so you can sleep well, and eat nourishing food that doesn't compromise your health or immune system.

One of the most effective ways to reduce stress is to delegate. When you've surrounded yourself with honest, trustworthy people, you won't have to do everything yourself. Find ways to coach people, so they will take on more duties without being overloaded, thus taking up some of your burdens.

As the ultimate decision-maker for the project team, you may sometimes be the one making the decisions, usually under conditions in which you don't know all the information perfectly. However, it will help both you and the team if you coach them through decisions when you can. It also helps team members hone their critical thinking skills. Note that it may mean a little more time spent on your side because you may have been able to make that choice pretty easily yourself. In the long run, however, having team members who can make those kinds of decisions will benefit you and free up your time.

Take comfort in how, if you can manage all this, everyone will hate you equally at the end of the project if you've done your job correctly!

"The best is the enemy of the good." —Voltaire

Given that we are all humans and, therefore, perfection isn't feasible, a project manager needs to focus on what's good enough. If you're continually trying to achieve perfection, you'll never be able to release something that satisfies the requirements. Besides, you will have a lot of items on your plate, and trying to give 100% on all of them won't be possible. Work on making it good enough, then move on. Remember that you are not delivering results to yourself, but to the stakeholders and their expectations.

You're probably familiar with the Pareto Principle, which says that 80% of the result is driven by 20% of the contribution. It's no less true for project management, which we can illustrate with the following three aspects.

- **Cost**

    Most of the expenses on any given project are due to salary or contract wages. People are the most pricy contributions to the budget, so make sure you're getting the bang for your buck. Choose talented, mature team members who will provide value for their labor.

    This also means that it's not the resource issue that's your enemy on a successful project. It's *time*. The better you can manage timelines, the more likely you will be to achieve your objectives. When you get your tasks done when they should be, you set a good example for the rest of the team.

- **Contributors**

    When it comes to your team, 20% of members will produce 80% of the work. Focus on these high performers and provide them the resources they need to perform at their best. You probably won't have enough time and money for the whole team, so make sure you are prioritizing your *star* workers.

- **Results**

    If you manage to get 80% of the goals targeted in the scope of work, congratulations! You've *completed* your project successfully. The key here is to focus on the activities and goals that have the highest return on investment. These will be ones that provide the biggest impact and get you closest to the overall goal.

With all of this, the joke is that projects are always 95% complete and never finished. Therefore, strive to be that rare PM who finishes one project and moves on to another. Hand it off, even if it's in project phase one, so you can then move on to project phase two.

Closing Out

Simply handing over the deliverables isn't always enough for a successful project. You want the changes you've made to stick, and for them to do so, you'll need to focus on closing tasks. You, the team, and the stakeholders have spent a lot of time and energy on the project; what a shame to waste it by not genuinely following through at the end to ensure the project results are safely in the hands of those who will benefit from and use them.

Not only that, but the team's credibility and reputation could be damaged if something goes wrong after the delivery. If the process change you implemented, for example, doesn't stick, it could be viewed as the team's fault. There are a couple of things that can go wrong when the closing process isn't handled correctly.

- **Orphan item**

    If the receiving team or department doesn't undergo the necessary training and awareness for the project's deliverable, they won't be able to use it. If you (or the project sponsor) didn't work through the buy-in process with the users of the deliverable, they wouldn't use it because they don't see the need for it, and probably feel like it's been foisted upon them.

    By contrast, when the users know why they're receiving the deliverable, have been trained on how to use it, and had input on the process, they will be more likely to take charge of it after the hand-off is done properly.

    Imagine you bought a brand-new computer, but no one at the store or the manufacturer could fix it when something went wrong. The project team may have developed it, but there was no training beyond the team on the new item. In this example, the store and manufacturer dropped all responsibility for it beyond adding it to the shelves.

- **The never-ending project**

    In this case, the organization continues to hold the project team accountable for operating and maintaining the deliverable, rather than the departments who should be taking responsibility. The receiving departments don't train or task their members to understand and operate the deliverable, leaving the project team responsible without the necessary capacity and skills to maintain it.

    Suppose you bought the brand-new computer, but every time you have a question about it, the manufacturer would send you back

to the project team. They built it, but they didn't load on the software or had anything to do with its creation, so they cannot answer your questions.

Also, as we've discussed, scope creep and the additions of extras keep the project going long after it should have been completed.

To avoid these scenarios, the project manager needs to close out the project thoroughly and ensure the transfer from the project team to the department is handled properly. There are three steps, which may seem obvious or trite (Aziz, 2015).[11] However, if you don't carry out and document them correctly, you could end up with unearned blame or reputation damage.

1. Declare all work has been completed

The PM should check in with the project sponsor and the customer and make sure they approved the delivered work. Any contracts (such as procurement) should be reviewed for completion and ensured both parties had executed them to the full extent of the agreement.

2. Assurance that all project processes have been achieved

Review the process and governance documents to ensure that they've been executed. Validate the achievement of business case objectives.

3. Formal agreement by all parties that the project is complete

Recognize that the project is complete and the transition of the deliverable to operations. Free the resources up from the project to begin work on other projects, or return to their functional teams.

Capture the lessons learned. This is especially important for the team members, who may have been unable to have a perspective on how the whole project operated. Recording lessons learned helps both the team members and stakeholders implement improvements in the future and avoid losing valuable information.

Sometimes You Have to "Take the L"

Just as you don't want to accept unwarranted blame, avoid doing the same to others. As you know, the buck stops with you as the project manager. If something doesn't go right and it's under the team's umbrella, you may have to *"take the L"* (loss).

Team members will get things wrong from time to time, as you do too. Good leaders look for the lesson in the mistakes and avoid overly harsh punishment. Empathy and rewards for good work go a lot farther than coercion or threats.

Will you need to call people out from time to time? Probably. If there's a lesson to be learned and the whole team needs to hear it, you often do need to put that person on the spot. However, you don't need to shame them in front of the team either.

When something goes wrong and you can fix it, do so. Even better is if you can coach the person who got it wrong on how to fix it. Either way, avoid the blame game and focus on getting the process back on track.

People are your biggest expense, and they're also your most significant resource. Deploy them to the best advantage of them and the team, with coaching to help them over the hurdles. When the team does hit a roadblock that the sponsor couldn't or didn't remove, don't panic. Work with your players to get around or over it if you can't move it.

Being a project manager requires a degree of maturity, which means you must avoid scapegoating. It doesn't matter who—don't blame the

client, sponsor, team member, or any stakeholders. Even if you think only your team will hear you, trust me, word gets around. Most often, it doesn't matter how you got to where you are now. What matters is the situation you're in and how you plan to get out of it and put the project back on track, so you can achieve your goals.

Key Takeaways

Completing the project on time is what you need to focus along the way, including how you handle the transition from the project team to operations.

- There is no such thing as project perfection, so work on being good enough and leverage the 80% to drive results.

- Handing off the deliverable properly affects the reputation of the team while ensuring that the work and lessons learned don't go to waste.

- Sometimes, you will need to take the loss, so learn from mistakes and move on without spending time shifting blame around.

In the next chapter, you will learn which technical skills you need to master.

---

[11] https://www.pmi.org/learning/library/importance-of-closing-process-group-9949

CHAPTER 7

TAKE COMMAND OF THE TECHNICAL SKILLS

WHILE it's true that project managers don't necessarily need to have the type of in-depth skill sets that members of the team do, you still need to master the capabilities required for an effective PM. The management of a project has its own requirements, which is where you are the expert and why firms want to hire you. Your team members are the masters of their specific domains, and you're the one who combines them and creates a structure for them to work at their best. However, your job doesn't end with organization and planning because you're the one who's held accountable for the success or failure.

Having said that, the more you understand what your team members are doing, the better. That will help you give an appropriate amount of time to the tasks and hire the right people for the work. It will also be easier to develop the project plan and evaluate performance when you have some knowledge of the benchmarks. If you work in software development, for example, knowing the fundamentals of coding will help you manage the project.

When there's a technical challenge, you'll be better equipped to step in if necessary. Ideally, you'd have someone trained to do that or learn on the job when needed. However, everyone, including the project manager, needs to do what they can to achieve the goal. If you were unable to hire as many team members as you would have preferred, you might be the one to patch over the gaps in skills where the others cannot.

Technical Skills

You probably are already aware that project management tools and approaches change regularly, so you need to stay on top of the project management industry and ensure that you're using the right tools for the job.

- **Project management methodology**

    The history of project management, at least formally, begins with traditional, or waterfall, management. In this style, the PM plans the entire project out from beginning to end and manages with a top-down approach. One project may take months or even years to result in the deliverable. The stakeholders have a chance to put in their two cents at the beginning, and only receive status updates until the end. Most tasks occur sequentially, and the next task must wait for the previous one to finish before it can get started.

The software industry developed a different methodology known as agile, though many other industries have discovered its benefits. It can respond much faster to changes in the environment and provides deliverables much quicker. The work occurs in iterations—or *sprints*—of no more than a month long, and the stakeholders stay involved during the entire process. The PM is often more of a player-coach than a top-down manager.

Some projects, especially those that can't tolerate much change in a plan, are better off with traditional, such as the construction of a bridge. Others that require fast adaptation, like IT projects, are better off with agile. As a PM, you'll need to understand the strengths and weaknesses of each and when they're used best.

The vast majority (97%) of software development firms use agile frameworks, though not all of their project teams are truly agile (Barker, 2019).[12] In the next section, we'll discuss the more popular frameworks that exist within agile.

- **Measurement approaches**

    Earned value management is a tool designed to measure the performance of the project. It enables the PM to see where the project has been, where it is now, and where it's going. Earned Value is also known as the budgeted cost of work performed (BCWP); planned value is where the project should be in terms of the budget as of today. By comparing the planned value, earned value, and actual value of the work up to that point in time, the project manager can estimate completion times and burn rates. It doesn't work on every project, and the data must be accurate for it to work correctly.

    Other approaches to the question of "Where are you on the project?" include using incremental milestones or tracking when the project reaches a certain point compared to the expected achievement date. If there are no milestones then a "start-finish" measurement allows for progress only when the project is complete.

Others more qualitative (and therefore less attractive to PMs and the stakeholders) include measuring the level of effort and individual judgment. On some projects, particularly the more complex ones, it may be difficult to use any of the other methods. In some cases, a combination of approaches will work best.

Whenever possible, try to quantify the progress as much as you can, even when the measure is not precise. This will help you protect yourself because a measure is a fact that cannot be doubted. Opinion, however, can change quickly, especially in adverse situations when people try to blame others.

- **Tools**

The more tasks can be automated, the better. Rather than wasting valuable time manually updating spreadsheets or Gantt charts, the team members and project manager can free up their time for decision making and problem solving.

There are many project management software tools available online that allow the entire team to collaborate, either online or in-person, from anywhere in the world. Any changes that someone makes to a task flows through all related items.

You may have heard some of the more popular ones, such as Trello, Asana, ClickUp, and JIRA. Most of them provide the ability to automate "old-school" tools such as Gantt charts, Work Breakdown Structure (WBS) diagrams, timelines, and mind maps.

Agile Project Management

Rather than being task-based like traditional project management, agile is focused on principles. In fact, there's a 12-statement manifesto that guides the thinking behind all agile projects. Four core values underpin every type of agile project:

1. People before processes.
2. Working prototypes instead of extensive documentation.
3. Collaboration with the client.
4. Adaptation rather than sticking to the plan.

These different values mean additional skills for project managers who are more used to waterfall management. Being able to communicate is much more important because the agile project manager is always in touch with team members and stakeholders. They need to know how to talk to people of various educations and backgrounds.

An agile PM is much more of a coach than a manager when dealing with their team members. Their job is not to plan everything out and determine who does what and when. Instead, they're there to empower their team members to take on the challenges and organize themselves.

The core values, especially of communication and collaboration, are fundamental for project managers to embed in their work. Even waterfall managers will see benefits when they coach their team members instead of continually managing them down. As a PM, you hire people because of their talent and ability to do the work, so don't interfere with that by micromanaging or commanding instead of encouraging.

Some types of agile don't even have a role called "project manager," though, in practice, the PM is still working with the team.

The most popular agile frameworks you may have heard of include the following.

- **Scrum**

    Over half of software development companies use this style, named after a rugby scrum (Barker, 2019).[13] The Scrum Master acts as a PM to a large extent and is a player-coach within the team.

- **Kanban**

    In this framework, the project manager can organize and track the progress using a visual Kanban board. It's flexible, and the guiding principle is to manage the flow of work. This will, in turn, allow for changes along the way, resulting in high-quality deliverables.

- **Six Sigma**

    Usually used for process improvements, Six Sigma reduces the probability of defects and minimizes variability. It can be applied for a wide variety of processes—not just those in manufacturing, though that is where Six Sigma started.

    Like Scrum, there are no project managers in Six Sigma. Leaders ascend from yellow belt as complete novices in the framework up through white, green, and black or master black belt. There are specific project items and experience required to move from level to level.

- **Extreme programming (XP)**

    This type of agile is explicitly aimed at software and providing high-quality applications that have been tested robustly. It also makes life better for the development team. This framework uses test-first programming rather than the usual process of writing code and then testing. It also involves pair programming, in which two people sit at one computer and code.

    There are no specific roles on the team because everyone is specifically cross-trained. However, new teams may bring in a coach who's experienced in XP to develop team members, which may be an appropriate role for a project manager.

You will find more details about agile approaches, principles, and success factors in my book *Become an Agile Project Manager*.

Embrace Automation

We touched on automation in the software tools discussion. Before all the software was widely available, many PMs hand-coded their Gantt charts and entered data manually in other tools, such as spreadsheets. Project managers who started earlier may be used to all this manual work, but there are distinct benefits to automating as much as you possibly can.

- **Highest and best use of resources**

    Going back to the Triple Constraint from the beginning of this book, every PM is limited in their resources, especially in terms of time and money. We also noted that people are both your best and most expensive resource. Using these precious resources to enter information manually or do other tasks that a computer can do better is simply a waste.

You weren't hired to update data; you were hired to oversee the entire project and, more importantly, make decisions and solve problems. You also didn't hire your team to work through spreadsheets. You hired them for their expertise, knowledge, and ability to get the work done.

Use your resources wisely, making the highest and best use of their time and your time.

- **Omitting omissions** *(and other errors)*

    Even the most detailed manual entry clerk can transpose numbers, leave out a part of the formula that causes everything else to be wrong, or forget a crucial step in their work.

    A computer does not make such errors. The applications need to be programmed correctly, of course, but once it's set up for success, it won't fail, get tired, or take a break right when you need something to be updated urgently.

- **Smoothing workflow**

    Many detailed procedures and checklists can still fail or cause problems if the hand-off from one task to another is delayed or omitted entirely. Sometimes, workers may not understand who they're supposed to tag for the next step. In other cases, they may not be in the office, or some other common circumstance occurred.

    Project management software allows for tasks to be owned, so when one is completed, the next owner can be notified automatically that their step is ready. Recent applications have advanced communication and storage tools that bring cooperation to another level of efficiency.

Backup Your Backups

During the planning phase, you should have identified some potential risks to the successful completion of the project. However, there will always be some unknown threats that no one sees coming, and you will need to have a flexible contingency plan for them. When they arise, stay calm and feel free to use your team and stakeholders to solve the problem.

Power outages and server issues are problems that everyone deals with from time to time, so your information needs to be backed up periodically. Most software providers offer this service, but you can also consider backing up on an external hard drive or some other source. What will you do if there's a natural disaster in the area? What if a team member is out sick for a significant period?

These are the types of things that hopefully won't happen, and you may not activate a plan when you don't need it. However, you will still need to have some ideas for what you'll do if they occur. For example, you may have other potential team members who can fill in for someone who will be out for a while. You wouldn't hire them just in case, but you would have their contact info in your proverbial back pocket should the need arise.

Always assume that something will go wrong because they will! Hopefully, whatever happens is not catastrophic to the project and, if you're lucky, you'll just have some mild irritations to deal with. However, you can't always count on such situations that happen only to be mild when wanting to ensure your project is a success. Thinking ahead and looking through the consequences of those consequences will help you manage through the ordeal.

"It must be remembered that project management is first and foremost a philosophy of management, not an elaborate set of tools and techniques. It will only be as effective as the people who use it." — Bryce's Law

Know Your Business

While having a fundamental knowledge of the project tasks and being an expert in project management is necessary, it won't be sufficient. The PM also needs to understand the industry in which they're working and the specific client who hired them for that project.

The PM must have a good grasp on the business case and how it impacts the organization and its business objectives. That helps the project manager assign priorities and know which of the two they're going to deliver—that being fast, cheap, or good. They understand the kinds of results their clients want to see, and can explain such to their team members as well.

To do that, however, the PM needs to understand the business itself. Who are its customers and what problems does the firm solve for them? What are the competitive advantages that give them a toehold over their competition, and what are the potential threats to the business? Even if your insight can't get too deep into their financials, you still need to understand where much of their profit comes from, along with their marketing, sales, and distribution efforts. This type of knowledge will also help you uncover the likely risks with the project, so you can plan to mitigate or avoid them if possible.

Knowledge of the industry is also helpful because you have an overview of the key players and their advantages and disadvantages. Step into the client's shoes and see who they would like to hire and the kinds of backgrounds they might prefer in a project manager.

Suppose you're looking for a project in the automotive industry in product development. If you were hiring a PM for your firm, would you rather employ someone who has worked in automotive before, or one whose specialty is in financials or IT?

You may be wondering how you can absorb this knowledge. Much of it is acquired over time. If you're a project manager who works within a specific organization, for example, you'll understand the industry better as you work on more projects.

Whether or not you are already working for the organization, you can always ask your project sponsor to help you fill in the blanks. Ask why this project specifically, about its timing, and how they expect it to impact the bottom line and their goals.

You'll also need to look for opportunities to learn about a particular company or field, depending on whether you plan to work for different organizations or just the one. If you don't have a chance at your current firm, consider volunteering in your community to get exposure, more knowledge, and more experience.

Key Takeaways

The project manager role requires a fundamental understanding of every position in the project, even if they're not subject-matter experts on the details. However, the PM must also be a master in project management and be able to choose the appropriate tools and techniques for their projects.

- As a project manager, you'll need to know the differences between waterfall and agile, which methods should be used on which projects, and stay up to date on performance measurement and other tools.

- Agile is a flexible methodology that allows for rapid changes and has been used increasingly by organizations all over the world.

- Automation helps PMs make the highest and best use of all their resources.

- Backing up information and creating contingency plans is necessary for every effective project manager.

- To be effective, PMs must also have a solid knowledge of the company and industry they're working in, so they can make the right decisions about the project.

In the next chapter, you will learn about taking your project management abilities to the next level.

---

[12] https://betanews.com/2019/05/07/state-of-agile-report/
[13] https://betanews.com/2019/05/07/state-of-agile-report/

CHAPTER 8

LEVEL UP YOUR PM GAME

RIGHT now, you should have a pretty good understanding of *what* effective PMs do. You've probably identified some areas in which you need to improve your knowledge or experience. In this chapter, we'll be talking about *how* project managers work to be more potent in managing successful projects.

Act with Integrity

Project managers can be seagulls, just like project sponsors or line managers; they could fly in, dump all over everything, then leave. Those types of PMs will find it difficult to maintain a career because word gets around. The smart and productive people who make up the team don't want to work for people like this, and they will turn down jobs. Project sponsors who hire PMs want a track record of accomplishments and good work habits.

The project manager that everyone wants to hire or work for is one whose career is based on honesty. This is the foundation for trust and relationships. People want to work with those who have strong morals and ethics and demonstrate them every day in their work. Empathy and interpersonal relationships are more important for leaders today than ever before, and only honest people can be authentic and genuine in their communications with others.

As a project manager, you're the role model for how the team behaves. If you don't act with integrity, neither will they. If you don't show that you're ethical in everything you do, neither will they. For the project to flow according to schedule, the team must work together. If they don't, there's very little chance of project success. Rather than completing their work, they'll end up shirking responsibilities. They lose the drive and motivation to make the highest quality deliverable possible because, with an unethical project manager, they will have no incentive to do their jobs. Team members with high morale often stand against unethical managers, and a lot of energy goes into internal fights for what is right and why it is important.

Doing what you said you would do is crucial for building good connections with your stakeholders and team members. If you say one thing and do another, why should anyone listen to what you have to say? Why should they trust you? Practicing what you preach is a key element in developing a strong and mature team. That's the kind of reputation that project managers want to have. When word gets around that you're a loyal PM who acts with integrity, you'll have plenty of offers from sponsors and colleagues who want to be a part of your next project.

Often, when you're working on a project and feeling stressed, you'll be tempted to bypass principles or rules and morals set by the company. However, a PM must act according to ethics and rules. If you try to

manipulate results, hide the bad news, or make excuses because "everybody else does it this way," no one will want to work with or hire you. It's selfish and irresponsible to set aside ethics. People see that you act in ways that would only benefit yourself, not team members, or the project as a whole when problems arise. And everyone knows that complications are common.

Reduce Red Tape

You'll likely find more bureaucracy in immature organizations. It's the project sponsors and senior management who don't really understand how projects work and why they're essential. They demand extensive documentation, project plans, status reports, long meetings, and a commission to decide everything, thus there ends up being no personal responsibility. Though, in all honesty, PMs can be bureaucrats too and allow the projects to be wound about with unnecessary rules and regulations.

When you can remove the bureaucracy as far away from your team as possible, you free them up to do their work. Automate as much as you can to create project documentation. Remember that you're fighting against time and have limited resources, so make the highest and best use of your resources that you can.

Be Organized

OK, you don't have to apply Marie Kondo's style to your workspace if that doesn't work for you. However, the more organized you can be in your work, the better. Don't let mess (either physical or mental) interfere with the smooth operation of your project.

You're the standard-bearer for your team members, just as you are when acting with integrity. If you're not organized, they have no incentive to be either. More importantly, if there's anyone on the team who needs to know where everything in the process is and where it should be, it's you. How much progress has been made since the last milestone, and is there a variance between that and the plan?

Tracking progress and performance is critical for success, so you can make small tweaks along the way, rather than a huge course correction if the variances are allowed to grow too large.

Time management is another component of being truly organized. For the team to do their best work, they can't be stressed or under too much pressure. Your job is to balance this with the needs of the project for productive hours as best you can. You've hired great people, so you shouldn't have to push them very hard. Guide and help them set priorities for what must be done on any given day, then let them figure out how to achieve that. It does require you, as the PM, to set the priorities effectively and communicate them.

Understanding People and Psychology

To get the most from your team players, it's helpful to know a little bit about what motivates workers in general and how each person works best. Can you be an effective PM without understanding psychology? Yes, if you can hire good people who are driven to do a good job. But leveling up your game requires more knowledge about what makes people tick, so you can leverage that to get the best work out of your people without stressing them out. Fundamentally, great people want to do a great job, so if you can help them do that, you will end up with excellent results. But there is more to it than that.

From reading this book, you know a few things you may not have before. We discussed that fear of change is built into the human psyche. Messages travel between two parts of the brain to compare what the brain expects from previous experience to what it sees now.

If those two things are different, the mind then believes that it's under threat and activates alarm systems. You know that you'll need to focus on everyone's favorite radio station, WII-FM, to help them through any changes by demonstrating how it benefits them.

People also have different drivers of behavior. You'll find some people are motivated solely by money and get the most out of monetary rewards. Others need to be praised regularly for the good jobs they do, so they can feel appreciated. Some people just want the facts and desire to find out the truth of the matter. Understanding how your team members are motivated will help you provide rewards for outstanding performance. Not everyone gets a trophy in project management, but you do want to recognize those who go above and beyond.

If you want to understand people's personalities, there are different ways to compare and contrast, some of which you're probably familiar with, or have at least heard of. Before assessing your team members and stakeholders, you have to understand yourself, who you are, what motivates you, what you dislike, and how you can improve your character.

The following measures are relative. Nobody is 100% one personality type, and nobody acts the same in all situations. However, certain patterns of our behavior may be dominant. It often happens that one is neutral; for example, someone could be neither an extrovert nor an introvert. The good news is that no personality is better or worse than another because each has its pros and cons.

Myers-Briggs (MBTI)[14]

This test is very popular. It measures personalities along four axes, meaning there are 16 possible personality types within its chart.

1. Extraversion/Introversion

They measure whether people are more comfortable in a crowd or by themselves. It's common to believe that introverts are shy, but they may be quite outgoing when they're with people they know and trust. They are often great analysts. Extroverts, on the other hand, find it easy to speak to people, though they may often overlook important details.

2. Sensing/Intuition

How do people take in information? The ones who are higher in sensing rely on facts and what they can see and touch. These are the team members who enjoy a hands-on experience. People who score higher in intuition; however, focus on patterns and expressions; they enjoy learning and talking about abstract theories.

3. Thinking/Feeling

This axis is based on how people prefer to make decisions. Interestingly, neuroscience has discovered that our subconscious is the one making the decisions, and we justify them after the fact.

Those who score higher on thinking weigh out the advantages and disadvantages of the options before making the final decision. You may see them listing pros and cons, for example. The members higher in the feeling attribute put more emphasis on whether the decision will promote harmony in the group and how others may feel about certain decisions before making theirs.

4. Judging/Perceiving

Don't get tricked by the words on this scale because they're misleading. A person high on the judging scale isn't necessarily judgmental; they merely prefer some structure and closure with their activities. By contrast, high perceivers are more flexible and open and don't necessarily focus on finishing a task.

The MBTI may be difficult for you to use in practice due to its high number of possibilities. On the other hand, many people are familiar with this particular personality test and may already know which type they are.

DISC[15]

There are only four personality types in this assessment. You can think of it as a 2x2 matrix, with one axis being activity (fast-paced vs. cautious), whereas the other is a continuum of trusting vs. skeptical.

1. Dominance

Fast-paced and skeptical, the D team member doesn't want to hear a long story. Let them know what you want from them directly. They may also be innovative and often argumentative.

2. Influence

These team members are fast-paced and trusting, also making them persuasive and emotional. They're the peacemaker of the team. While they may sometimes be more concerned with popularity than the right decisions, they encourage the rest of the team.

3. Steadiness

Trusting and cautious, these team members are strong team players and good listeners. They tend to struggle with change, but they are still very dependable in their work.

4. Compliant

Don't be fooled by the name, as these team members are merely cautious and skeptical, not necessarily submissive to authority.

They're logical and analytical. Though they can get easily bogged down in the details, they don't like to argue either.

The DISC system has the benefit of being easy to remember, and you can probably eyeball your team members and determine where they would fall along each axis without too much effort.

Big Five (OCEAN)[16]

Psychologists often consider these the five factors—dubbed by its acronym "OCEAN"—determine a person's behavior most above other tests. As with the other tests described above, it is believed that people exist on a continuum for each of these factors. Understanding where they are on each aspect will help you determine how to work with them more effectively.

1. Openness to experience

This includes creativity and intellectual curiosity. Creative people are often good problem solvers because they can think outside the proverbial box.

2. Conscientiousness

This aspect measures how likely someone is to finish what they start, how responsible they feel toward their work, and how productive they may be. You definitely want people who are high on this scale on your team.

3. Extroversion

This scale is defined a little differently from the MBTI scale, though its opposite is still introversion. This scale measures assertiveness and sociability.

4. Agreeableness

How much does someone trust other people? Are they compassionate and respectful? Having a team in which the members are higher in agreeableness will encourage them to work together.

5. Neuroticism

This trait looks at how much the person's tendencies may lean them toward developing depression or anxiety.

In reality, you won't have time to delve too deep into your team players psychologically. However, you can get a reasonable understanding of whether they play well with others, run with scissors, and how they can be motivated during the time you spend with them.

If you recognize specific patterns in their behavior, you can reallocate tasks. One team member may be fit for gathering and processing data quickly. In contrast, another may be better for analytical work and decision-making, and someone else may be best for persuading others. In other cases, someone could be a great worker who needs just a few instructions, whereas another person could be a great negotiator who can improve harmony among the team.

Set, Manage, and Never Give Up on Your Expectations

People work best when they know what you want from them. At the outset of the project, this may be more difficult because it will evolve as you settle in and get to know all the players better. You also need to be firm on the expectations you have of the stakeholders, particularly on agile projects where you will be seeking feedback regularly. Also, set the expectations as early as possible in terms of what they can expect from you and the team.

When people come to you with questions, make sure they're within the scope of the work you agreed to. Otherwise, you could end up with the dreaded scope creep. If it's not your area of expertise and you don't know the answer, bring in your subject matter masters and let them handle it. If you don't have one at hand right when someone's asking you the question, that's OK. Just make sure you understand the question, follow up with the expert, then get back to the person with the question in a timely fashion.

You know you can't deliver the moon, so make sure you don't promise it upfront. That makes managing the expectations much more comfortable. Your communication skills are helpful here because you may need to adjust the deliverable or action as you go along. Although you may do your best to mitigate all issues, not all of them will be solvable, and you will need to communicate that. Again, do so in a timely fashion, not waiting until the end of the project and delivering something different from what was promised.

Don't let go of your expectations. If you set the standard for quality of work and it starts slipping, don't let it go. If the team has a required check-in with a stakeholder regularly, ensure it doesn't fall through the cracks. That includes any standards you've set for yourself—don't allow yourself to fall below them in the interest of expediency. Getting back to acting with integrity, you must do what you say you're going to do.

Be Your Project Team's Biggest Fan

We discussed earlier that, as a project manager, you're the one responsible for clearing roadblocks for your team and not allowing them to be pressured by stakeholders or anyone else. The more you anticipate questions or issues from your stakeholders, the more you can clear the way for your team.

At the same time, you will want the team to do their best work. That could mean challenging them on occasion, or asking if they've thought of an alternative solution to a problem. Don't let them give up on a tough task or get discouraged when an ordeal seems to be more difficult than everyone thought at first. Celebrate the wins and continue to encourage and coach during the entire project.

Demonstrate your support of the team and the process. Doing so sets the tone for stakeholders, so they too can take pride in the effort of the team. Likewise, it also encourages your team as well. When they know you have their backs, they will be more likely to put in that extra effort that often results in breakthroughs or superior products.

Key Takeaways

You don't have to be an ordinary effective project manager, but, with some additional tweaks, you can become next-level in your performance.

- Acting with integrity is a crucial behavior that you need if you want to be hired by preferred organizations and work with great team members.
- The more red tape you can remove from the process, the better.
- Being organized in time and space allows you to maximize the resources available to you.
- Understanding what makes your team players tick will help you motivate and work with them.
- Make sure you set appropriate expectations that you can maintain and hold onto throughout the entire project.
- Your project team needs a big fan, and that fan is *you*.

In the next chapter, you will learn how to up your game consistently with continuous improvement.

---

[14] https://www.verywellmind.com/the-myers-briggs-type-indicator-2795583
[15] https://discinsights.com/disc-theory
[16] https://www.psychologytoday.com/us/basics/big-5-personality-traits

CHAPTER 9

ALWAYS BE IMPROVING

CONTINUOUS learning is critical for becoming an effective project manager and maintaining that effectiveness. Technology is continually changing, and there are always new developments and circumstances on the horizon. Successful PMs enjoy learning new things anyway, and it's good for the brain too. Being able to learn from each experience, then applying those lessons will only help you master the skills of project management.

Curiosity

When everything changes regularly, there will always be questions asked to illuminate how those changes affect your work. Get to know the company and the reasons behind the project. Also, understand what's going on in the broader world that affects your project and your company.

For example, who are the key players in the industry? What are the new technologies being developed? What are the pressures on the industry as a whole and the company in particular? Think about the supply chain for resources for your project. Who are the major suppliers? Who are their competitors and what pressures are they facing?

There's always more to know. As a project manager, you'll never get to a point where you can say to yourself: *I know everything there is to know about this project, company, and industry.* On the other hand, if you ever do, recognize you are missing something. Some new technology you never dreamed of may appear on the scene to automate or speed up a process that you're using. A new player might emerge, or another project manager in your company may bring a better project management tool or process.

Staying curious keeps you sharp. It ensures that you're always looking to see what's new and improved, which means you can make your project even better. Besides, your career will grow as well.

Lessons Learned

At the end of the project, or sprint/iteration in agile, make sure the team and stakeholders meet to discuss lessons learned and document them. Making sure the teachings don't get lost is crucial for implementing changes and truly improving later. Identifying what went wrong is only the first step; the only way to get *better* is to use those learnings in the future.

At one company I worked for, the process was called "Plus/EBIs." At the meeting, someone would get out the easel and paper and write down the lessons. To avoid shaming and blaming, each person who spoke would note a Plus, which was something that went well, before naming an EBI: "Even Better If." EBIs were things that went wrong and how to avoid them for the next time.

Does it seem a bit silly to ensure that a Plus gets written down? It's not, specifically for reasons of morale, that you will want to indicate the things that went right. These are also lessons that can be transferred to future projects. Maybe the team discovered a new way of doing something that had positive results, or it was a method that allowed everyone to work to their full potential.

In addition to the "don'ts," people need to know what to do. They need to know what does work instead of wasting time figuring it out. Remember that you're trying to maximize your resources on all projects—if you know something works well, why wouldn't you want to copy it and use it for the next one? Documenting that resource ensures it's not forgotten months from when you created it.

Cognitive Skills

This is the type of intelligence that's applied to the ability to plan, think critically, and solve problems. It also provides the foundation for being able to learn from experience and apply it to new situations.

Effective PMs must know how to analyze the data they have, even though it is likely incomplete, and make decisions based on that imperfect information. As you work on more projects, you'll end up with higher complexity that you must manage on behalf of your team and stakeholders.

Being able to handle increasing amounts of complexity doesn't necessarily mean you need to have any kind of college degree, as long as you can think analytically and be a leader. There are certificates that you can attain, such as the Project Management Professional (PMP) issued by the Project Management Institute and recognized around the world (PMI, n.d.)[17]. If you're using Six Sigma as your methodology, various institutions issue Green and Black belts according to your experience. I, myself, am a Green belt, but I don't work on many Six Sigma projects. Other certifications are available, such as Scrum Master, as well.

Some organizations may require their project managers to have or obtain one of these designations, but not all do. They're helpful when you're starting and don't have a significant track record for project sponsors to look at because they know you've at least been trained in the methodology. If you've been in the project management arena for some time and have a solid background in the methodology already, you may not need the certification.

Being a project manager is not about degrees and certifications; it's about your skills and capabilities. That is, how well you communicate and think through problems to arrive at a solution, along with your ability to manage a team and other resources. If you don't have a college degree, experience counts for a lot in this field. Sponsors are looking explicitly for results. A project manager who can plan, analyze, deliver, and, most importantly, learn from previous projects and apply the lessons, is a star.

Continuous Improvement

Have you heard that a shark has to keep swimming or it will die? Project managers must keep improving or their careers will die. Effective PMs are interested in self-development and want to continue learning and getting better at their jobs anyway, even if it didn't have a significant impact on their careers. Invariably, it does.

Building your proficiency as a project manager is not only about the technical skills of project management, learning about new performance measurement tools, or project management software. Beyond those mentioned, it encompasses leadership qualities, which can always be improved.

Look for ways that you can work on all these skills. Obviously, projects are a vital way to improve your craft! However, you should consider other opportunities as well. You might take a course, either online or at the college campus. Remember, you don't need an MBA. Community colleges offer classes on these topics, and many project management organizations have online courses you can take anytime.

One great thing about increasing your leadership capabilities is that every community has plenty of organizations and positions where you can work on them. Volunteering allows you to interact with all kinds of different people so that you can practice your communication abilities as well.

Mentors who can guide you in your career and answer questions about the field can be extremely helpful. If your human resources department offers mentoring, take them up on it! Otherwise, look for a role model whom you would like to emulate in your work. If they aren't close to you geographically, you can have an online relationship too. That person can be from a different background than project management. However, what's important is their attitude and maturity in skills that are important to you.

Some people don't like the word "mentor" because they believe it implies a lot of work and commitment on their part. Thus, you may not want to walk up to someone and ask them bluntly to be your mentor. However, making a *commitment* is critical if you really want to achieve anything valuable in your career and life.

Organizational Training Plan

When working for a mature firm that builds the value of project management into their budget, they will have training for every employee. This will even be so for workers who may not be working on projects. It's still essential for them to understand the value of it and how it adds to the goals. Not everyone will undergo the same training, of course. Project managers may need to know how to build an effective team or use advanced project management features, but other employees and executives won't.

In mature organizations, each role has its own training plan. The instruction is tailored to the individual and aligned with business objectives. No training for training's sake, but each employee will have the guidance or a training plan necessary for their particular contribution to the firm. That way, everyone involved has a foundation of knowledge that supports all programs and projects. Such a training program requires resources from the organization.

The training plan must have a budget and a schedule for every team member to be trained. Not all of the training is necessarily cost-related, because some aspects, such as coaching, typically don't require a line item on the budget. The team would include all the executives (including the C-suite), upper management, line management, and employees. The plan itself is aligned with the business plan and objectives, along with the projects and programs that will allow the company to achieve its goals.

Fortunately for all, we live in the 21st century, so there are a variety of training options to choose from. Online training, onsite training, study materials, coaching, and mentoring are just a few delivery mechanisms available. They range from one-off training up to a whole education system. The trainers may be contracted out or located in-house. In addition to the new employee training that everyone would receive, a mature organization also ensures access to continuous learning.

Last, but certainly not least, the firm's training plan must include metrics around performance and benefits or goals achieved. There is no point in maintaining a training plan that isn't fruitful. Maybe the organization measures improvement in project performance as

a result of the training, or value generated. The metrics are refined in conjunction with an annual review of the plan to see if any changes need to be made.

If you're not working for a mature organization that lays a training plan out for its project managers specifically, check with your management to see if any of these training packages are available. As noted earlier, the experience is vital for a PM. Still, continuous improvement requires target training that helps you improve on technical and leadership project management skills, as well as business and broader knowledge. Ensure that you block out time on your schedule that will be dedicated to training.

What if your organization doesn't offer training? That doesn't mean you get to skip it. You'll need to do research on your own (or have a team member do it) to find a package that will improve your skills and that of your team players. You must dedicate time for all to get better at their project management capabilities.

If you want to bring project management to the next level in your organization, explain the reasons and benefits, then propose some options to your management. Most executives do not know what project management skills must be developed. However, you have this knowledge, and if you explain the benefits and how the firm will achieve better results than ever before, you can win their buy-in.

Measuring Training's Return On Investment (ROI)

With massive amounts spent on training, depending on the size of the organization, there must be a measurable ROI to justify the expense for profit-conscious entities. ROI modeling is a systematic approach to comparing the cost of training to its benefit, and choosing programs that result in the biggest bang for your buck.

It starts with the training plan, which must be tied directly to the firm's business plan. The blueprint specifies the goals of the training, which should link back to the business objectives, the investment or budget, and the anticipated benefits. It bridges the current skills of employees and managers to the vision, where the firm initiates and implements projects successfully.

How can you best indicate the value of the training? The easiest way to measure is to send out a survey to the participants afterward, but this is entirely subjective and doesn't give any meaningful feedback as to the benefits of the training. Final exams measure the individual employee's learning as a result of the training, which is at least objective. However, they still don't address the actual value or effects to the bottom line. They only measure the performance of the trainer, the quality of training materials, and how much the employees learned.

A concrete way to test the benefits is to put the training to work, where the value measurement is implemented and tracked for a few months after the training to ensure that improvement actually takes place. Typical measures include productivity, error rates, and velocity. This is the best way for companies to determine whether they're benefiting from the training plan.

Project Manager-Specific Training

Effective PMs balance business, technical, and leadership skills, so their training must encompass all three. As you know, training won't get you all the way to effectiveness, but it is a key component of continuous growth. As a project sponsor myself, I looked for the experience and track record—not just the degrees or certificates potential PMs had attained. I also made sure that I saw time dedicated to learning and growing.

I didn't want project managers who'd taken a training course or two and thought that was all they needed. To make my projects successful, I knew I needed those who continued to learn and wanted to get better, whether their organization supported that or not.

At the entry level—for those just starting—sponsors expect to see a base of knowledge of project management, as well as problem-solving skills. The training that project managers require at this level include:

- Fundamentals of project management, including methods and reporting.
- Problem-solving.
- Managing conflicts.

One step up from entry level is where the project manager will need more leadership skills because projects are a bit more complex, as well as a step up in technical competence, including an understanding of best practices in project management. At this stage, they should know more about the business as well. As you would expect, the training goes deeper now.

- Tools and best practices.
- Active listening.
- Developing relationships.
- Team building.
- Organizational Project Management (OPM) framework.
- Cognitive intelligence.
- Business knowledge.

PMs at the advanced level learn program management tools and techniques, where a program is a large project consisting of smaller interdependent projects. Their leadership and business proficiency is more advanced, and they are capable of leading global or virtual teams.

- Improving EQ (emotional intelligence).
- Facilitation, mentoring, and coaching.
- Negotiation.
- Empowering and setting direction.
- Project financials.
- Global projects with distributed teams.
- Performance management.
- Organizational Change Management.

On the next level of senior project managers, the PMs understand and leverage the OPM framework, including the details of the business plan and how programs and projects deliver value to the business.

- Business planning.
- Value management.
- Program management and performance.

Finally, at the strategic level, a PM is involved in creating the business plan and generating value across the entire portfolio of programs and projects.

- Strategic business planning.
- Managing the portfolio of programs and projects.
- Portfolio performance management.

Each level builds on the one below it, and the PM must master every level through training and experience before ascending to the next.

You can see that, as you grow through the stages of project management, your technical, leadership, and business capabilities develop in complexity as well. Training at each level needs to support the goals of that stage effectively for a project manager to improve.

Finding a project manager role when you have the training but not the experience can be difficult. To overcome this, you can ask your manager to lead a small project for the group, or be assigned to a larger project and assist that PM with some of the management tasks. Another way to build these proficiencies is to assist a nonprofit or volunteer group with taking charge of an event. You can also search for companies that are offering entry-level PM employment or freelance jobs and apply for them. You need to combine your training with practice to grow as a project manager.

Remember that projects typically grow in complexity as they do size-wise. Don't assume that just because you successfully led a small project that you're ready to tackle a much larger one. Build on your skills and take the lessons learned from each project for the next one, and, over time, you'll have the experience and knowledge necessary to excel at leading larger projects. It's better to have a track record of success that you develop one step at a time, rather than biting off a bigger project than you can chew and damaging your reputation as a result. Project management isn't going anywhere. In fact, it's expanding as more organizations become mature and see portfolios of projects as good ways to add to the bottom line. There will always be another project to work on, as long as you can show good results to those looking to hire PMs.

Key Takeaways

Being an effective project manager means continuous learning and improving. Situations are always changing, so staying on top of them is a challenge to accept. Training plans are vital for improving the team's project management skills, and each level has a more complex skill set that must be mastered.

- Curiosity may not be right for cats, but it's necessary for PMs who want to grow in their careers.

- At the end of each project or iteration, the team and stakeholders must gather to capture the lessons learned so they can be implemented for the next one.

- Project managers need to develop their cognitive intelligence as well.

- Effective project management relies on continuous improvement from the team members, especially the PM.

- Mature organizations already have a training plan in place for all employees with dedicated funds, but project managers in other firms must seek out opportunities for team training.

- As project managers grow in their careers, their knowledge and training requirements grow in complexity.

---

[17] https://www.pmi.org/certifications

FINAL WORDS

NOW that you've reached the end of this book, you should have a good grasp of what makes an effective project manager. You need to combine technical, leadership, and business skills to complete challenging projects successfully. As you develop through the different stages of being a PM, you'll need more advanced capabilities and training.

We talked about how to start as an effective project manager. There are different capabilities required, such as being able to communicate at all levels of business and prioritize issues for yourself and the team. Projects operate under the Triple Constraint of time, scope, and cost. These three are challenging to balance, but your job, as a project manager, is to try to keep them proportional to the objectives that the client has. You're the one who is responsible for the success or failure of the project, and the one who will be held accountable to a large extent. All the team members, stakeholders, tasks, and deliverables are puzzle pieces, with you being the one who fits them together and communicates the overall vision of the project.

The key elements of a project include a focus on value creation and the maintenance of scope, so you don't end up with the dreaded scope creep. Done is better than perfect, and you are the one driving the completion. That relies on your ability to plan and commit to the project properly. Unfortunately, none of us live in an ideal world, so you will also need to be able to manage risks appropriately. You may see some threats coming as you look out across the horizon, but others may be unexpected. You can't sit back and wait for them to happen; instead, be proactive in countering them.

Competency as a project manager is essential, and some of that will develop the more projects you manage. At the beginning of it, you'll find it helpful to discover what your client is an expert in. Valuing the client is critical for working well with them. Effective PMs have solid technical skills, and they also provide the vision that the team and stakeholders work towards. They set the direction for the team, but they don't micromanage. Instead, they empower team members to get the work done in a way that leverages their strengths.

In addition to a team that works well together under the PM's direction, a successful project has buy-in from client management at all levels, from the senior executives on down to the line. These managers demonstrate their support and provide resources as requested. Mature organizations have project management built into their business plans, and the projects align with business objectives. Everyone within the firm understands what's in it for them and acts accordingly.

Not all firms are mature when it comes to project management, and many PMs will find that they need to do the work to show management specific benefits of the project, and help them understand how they can demonstrate support. Organizational culture varies from those who value project management to those with negative attitudes or with little knowledge about it. PMs may find themselves assisting with organizational change management (OCM) to further their projects and have a better chance of success.

When the project manager has a project sponsor who understands, values, and supports their efforts, they also have a much higher chance of success. The sponsor is the one who owns and will champion the project. Best practices for PMs include meeting regularly with their sponsor and sitting down at the onset of the project to divide up responsibilities and ensure nothing is omitted. Mature firms will have effective sponsors for their projects, but project managers working outside those firms may need to help develop their sponsors into being the right kind of champions for the project.

Although PMs empower their teams, they also need to understand the various tasks and get down in the trenches with their team members when necessary. Planning the project isn't enough. The project manager must also see to its execution and properly closing out of

the project. They ensure a solid transition from the project team to operations, such that the receiving team is trained on the deliverable and understands the value of it; otherwise, the project might die on the vine. If operations never takes ownership, all questions come back to the project team, who aren't equipped to handle the ongoing process. Whether the project is successful or not, the PM should avoid playing the blame game and help the team overcome obstacles.

Having excellent technical skills will help you prevent some of those obstacles in the first place. You need to understand the different methodologies and the pros and cons of each, as well as ways to measure project performance. You'll step in when necessary, so you need some knowledge of the team members' capabilities, which they bring to bear on the project. You know you need to maximize your resources, and automating and backing up processes will help you deliver on schedule. In addition, to be most effective, you'll need to understand the business you're working in and its strengths and weaknesses, as well as potential opportunities and threats.

So far, so good. However, if you want to level up your game, you can go even farther. Always act with integrity, and you'll find hiring managers and team members who will want to work with you. Reduce red tape and be as organized as you can, so you can use your resources efficiently.

A key trait for effective PMs is the desire for continuous learning. You're always curious and trying to learn more about your craft, field, and company. At the end of a sprint or project, you would gather the stakeholders and team together to document the lessons learned, both positive and negative. Then, you will put that knowledge into action in future projects.

As an effective project manager, you would continue to obtain training for you and the team. Mature organizations have training plans and budgets, but you may need to do the research and develop one when you're not working for a mature firm. As you progress through the stages of being a project manager, from entry-level to strategic, your training will become more advanced. Although experience is important, training keeps you at the top of your game.

If you only take one idea away from this book, I hope it's the recognition that you can be effective without necessarily adding any degrees or certifications, and that you can get additional PM experience. Training does help you hone your natural talents and provides a structured method for improving your skills, yet you just need to start with the willingness to be teachable and a desire to grow and learn throughout your career.

Take what you've learned here and apply it, but also pass it on to your juniors. The more competent project managers the world has, the better. Now, you have the knowledge to go forth and be an even more effective project manager.

REFERENCES

Ali, J. (2017, December 21). *7 Tips on How to be a great Project Manager.* Retrieved from https://www.projecttimes.com/articles/7-tips-on-how-to-be-a-great-project-manager.html

Aston, B. (2020, April 29). *Essential Project Management Skills For 2020 (+How To Build Them).* Retrieved from https://thedigitalprojectmanager.com/project-management-skills/#soft-skills

Aziz, E. (2015, October 10). *Project Closing.* Retrieved from https://www.pmi.org/learning/library/importance-of-closing-process-group-9949

Barker, I. (2019, May 7). *97 percent of companies now use agile development methods.* Retrieved from https://betanews.com/2019/05/07/state-of-agile-report/

Bryce, T. (2006). *Why Does Project Management Fail?* Retrieved from https://www.projectsmart.co.uk/why-does-project-management-fail.php

Business Dictionary. (n.d.). *What is the Peter principle? definition and meaning.* Retrieved from http://www.businessdictionary.com/definition/Peter-principle.html

Cherry, K. (2019, July 17). *Myers-Briggs Type Indicator: The 16 Personality Types.* Retrieved from https://www.verywellmind.com/the-myers-briggs-type-indicator-2795583

CMOE. (2020, May 4). *5 Ways To Improve Your Strategic Thinking Skills Today.* Retrieved from https://cmoe.com/blog/improve-strategic-thinking-skills/

Colman, H. (2020, April 29). *Employee Training Metrics: How to Measure eLearning Effectiveness.* Retrieved from https://www.ispringsolutions.com/blog/training-metrics-how-to-measure-elearning-effectiveness

Curtis, L. (2019, October 26). *Five Must Have Core Competencies for Project Managers.* Retrieved from https://www.mpug.com/articles/five-must-have-core-competencies-for-project-managers/

DISC Insights. (n.d.). *DISC Theory and DISC Personality Traits.* Retrieved from https://discinsights.com/disc-theory

Florida Tech. (n.d.). *The Importance of Organizational Culture to Project Management.* Retrieved from https://www.floridatechonline.com/blog/business/the-importance-of-organizational-culture-to-project-management/

Gay, B. (2018, October 3). *What it Takes to be an Effective Project Manager.* Retrieved from https://www.projecttimes.com/articles/what-it-takes-to-be-an-effective-project-manager.html

Gilbert, J. (2012, March 27). *The Change Management Life Cycle; Involve Your People to Ensure Success.* Retrieved from https://www.batimes.com/articles/the-change-management-life-cycle-involve-your-people-to-ensure-success.html

Harned, B. (n.d.). *How to Become a Successful Project Manager.* Retrieved from https://www.teamgantt.com/guide-to-project-management

Harrin, E. (2018, December 17). **15 Essential Skills Every Project Manager Needs.** Retrieved from https://www.strategyex.co.uk/blog/pmoperspectives/15-skills-project-managers-will-need-2015/

Haughey, D. (2020, May 24). **Stop Scope Creep Running Away With Your Project.** Retrieved from https://www.projectsmart.co.uk/stop-scope-creep-running-away-with-your-project.php

Haughey, D. (2011, December 19). **Understanding the Project Management Triple Constraint.** Retrieved from https://www.projectsmart.co.uk/understanding-the-project-management-triple-constraint.php

HBS Online. (2017, November 2). **A 3-Step Change Management Framework for Businesses.** Retrieved from https://online.hbs.edu/blog/post/a-3-step-framework-for-managing-organizational-change

James, V. (2013, October 29). **Strategies for Project Sponsorship.** Retrieved from https://www.pmi.org/learning/library/strategies-project-sponsorship-5875

Kerzner, H. R. (2009). **Project Management Case Studies (3rd ed.).** New York, NY: Wiley.

KonMari. (n.d.). **About KonMari | The Official Website of Marie Kondo.** Retrieved from https://shop.konmari.com/pages/about

Leadem, R. (2018, August 12). **Why Emotional Intelligence Is Crucial for Success (Infographic).** Retrieved from https://www.entrepreneur.com/article/318187

Malsam, W. (2020, February 11). **What Is a Project Sponsor? Defining This PM Role.** Retrieved from https://www.projectmanager.com/blog/what-is-a-project-sponsor

May, A. (2016, December 14). **Stakeholder Buy-In: The Secret to Project Success.** Retrieved from https://www.dashe.com/blog/the-importance-of-stakeholder-buy-in

PM Tips. (2019, October 15). **Effective Project Leadership and Stress.** Retrieved from https://pmtips.net/article/effective-project-leadership-and-stress

Project Management Institute. (2018). **The Standard for Organizational Project Management.** Retrieved from https://www.pmi.org/pmbok-guide-standards/foundational/organizational-project-management

Psychology Today. (n.d.). **Big 5 Personality Traits.** Retrieved from https://www.psychologytoday.com/us/basics/big-5-personality-traits

Reichel, C. (2006). **Earned Value Management Systems (EVMS).** Retrieved from https://www.pmi.org/learning/library/earned-value-management-systems-analysis-8026

Santos, I. A. M. dos, Barriga, G. D. C., Jugend, D., & Cauchick-Miguel, P. A. (2019). **Organizational factors influencing project success: an assessment in the automotive industry, Production vol. 29.** Retrieved from https://doi.org/10.1590/0103-6513.20180108

Schibi, O., & Lee, C. (2015, October 10). **Project Sponsorship.** Retrieved from https://www.pmi.org/learning/library/importance-of-project-sponsorship-9946

Shenoy, A. (2014, January 29). **Bringing Vision to Your Projects: How to Excel as a Project Manager.** Retrieved from https://www.projecttimes.com/articles/bringing-vision-to-your-projects-how-to-excel-as-a-project-manager.html

Suda, L. V. (2007). **The Meaning and Importance of Culture for Project Success.** Retrieved from https://www.pmi.org/learning/library/meaning-importance-culture-project-success-7361

van Rooy, D. (2020, February 6). **7 Ways to Adopt a Proactive Mindset - and Achieve Success.** Retrieved from https://www.inc.com/david-van-rooy/7-ways-to-adopt-a-proactive-mindset.html

Wikipedia contributors. (2020, May 25). **Peter principle.** Retrieved from https://en.wikipedia.org/wiki/Peter_principle

Wikipedia contributors. (2020, April 1). **Seagull management.** Retrieved from https://en.wikipedia.org/wiki/Seagull_management

Windsor, G. (2020, March 3). **How to Work Effectively with Your Project Sponsor.** Retrieved from https://www.brightwork.com/blog/work-effectively-project-sponsor

Wrike. (n.d.). **What Is Portfolio in Project Management.** Retrieved from https://www.wrike.com/project-management-guide/faq/what-is-portfolio-in-project-management/

Wrike. (n.d.). **What is Program Management vs. Project Management?** Retrieved from https://www.wrike.com/project-management-guide/faq/what-is-program-management-vs-project-management/

Zilicus. (n.d.). **A Project Leadership Or Project Management - Becoming Effective Project Leader - Part II.** Retrieved from http://zilicus.com/Resources/blog-2014/Project-Leadership-Or-Project-Management-Becoming-Effective-Project-Leader-Part-ii.html

GLOSSARY AND ABBREVIATIONS

Agile/APM: Agile Project Management, methodology, or framework .... ch. 1
Agile Manifesto: 12 core values of APM defined in 2001 .... ch. 7
Analysis paralysis: Overthinking; not allowing decision making .... ch. 2
BCWP: Budgeted Cost of Work Performed (aka earned value) .... ch. 7
Black Belt/Master Black Belt: Six Sigma certification .... ch. 1
CCO: Chief Communications Officer .... ch. 4
CEO: Chief Executive Officer .... ch. 4
CPC: Cost Per Click (measurement of advertising expenses) .... ch. 4
DISC: Dominance, Influence, Steadiness, Compliant (personality types) .... ch. 8
EQ: Emotional Intelligence (understanding and managing emotions) .... ch. 1
Gantt Chart: A visual scheduling diagram named by Henry Gantt .... ch. 7
Global project: A project with members in different locations .... ch. 9
Jack of All Trades: Someone who is decent at everything .... ch. 1
Kanban: APM method for improving workflow; uses visual tools .... ch. 7
KPIs: Key Performance Indicators .... ch. 4
Leadership: A combination of skills, characteristics, and behaviors .... ch. 3
Marie Kondo: Wrote books about organizing, known as KonMari method .... ch. 1
MBTI: Myers-Briggs Type Indicator (personality types) .... ch. 8
Metrics: A system or set of measures, such as profitability, effectiveness .... ch. 4
MQ: Managerial Intelligence (management skills) .... ch. 1
OCEAN: Five personality type factors .... ch. 8
OPM: Organizational Project Management .... ch. 9
Organizational culture: employees' attitudes, behaviors, and values .... ch. 4
Plus/EBIs: Plus and Even Better Ifs (APM improvement practice) .... ch. 9
PM: Project Manager .... ch. 1
PMI: Project Management Institute .... ch. 9
PMP: Project Management Professional, certification .... ch. 9
Portfolio: Groups programs and projects .... ch. 4
Program: Consists of a group of related projects .... ch. 4
Project Manager: Leads the project and project team .... ch. 1
Risk Management: Foreseeing and addressing potential risks .... ch. 2
ROI: Return on Investment (return per dollar invested in the project) .... ch. 4
Scope Creep: Continuously adding new deliverables to the scope .... ch. 2
Scrum: The most popular APM method for developing complex products .... ch. 7
Scrum Master: A coach, promotes productivity, can be a project manager .... ch. 7
Six Sigma: A process improvement framework using statistics measures .... ch. 7
Sponsor: Has the most significant interest in the project's outcome .... ch. 5
Sprint: An iteration or cycle in the APM that lasts about a month .... ch. 7
Stakeholder: Has a share in the outcome of the project .... ch. 1
Triple Constraint triangle: Project limitations—cost, time, scope .... ch. 1
VP: Vice-President .... ch. 4
Waterfall: A traditional PM methodology; the chart resembles a waterfall .... ch. 1
WBS: Work Breakdown Structure (a tree structure with activities) .... ch. 7
WII-FM: What's In It For Me or Them (a way of communication) .... ch. 4
XP: Extreme Programming, an APM framework for software development .... ch. 7

BONUS: YOUR NEGOTIATION CHECKLIST

READY SET AGILE!

BEING A PROJECT LEADER

*Quick Guide
to Best Management Practices
and How You Can Excel
as a Successful
Project Manager*

INTRODUCTION

PROJECT managers are ultimately responsible for the success of their projects. They have to work with a variety of stakeholders, from team members to clients. Their technical skills have been honed from all their experiences on projects: estimating how long the project will take, what it will cost, and the necessary tasks and skills required to complete those tasks. By now, they've shown their capabilities as managers and are ready to go to the next level. Although technical skills and general management capabilities are required to become a successful project leader, they're not sufficient.

In the first book of this bundle, I discussed briefly the difference between being a manager and being a leader. You, as an aspiring project manager, are ready to take that next step to become a sought-after *leader*, moving up from *management*. Yet being a leader involves several *soft* skills that will serve you well in any kind of leadership position in the modern world and in your personal life.

Many problems you've faced require the application of new capabilities, particularly in interpersonal relations. Maybe you're having difficulties with individual personalities on the team being unable to work well together, or you're seeing many conflicts within or between the team and the client.

Communicating well is a skill. Although everyone learns to talk when they're young, as you know, the business world requires more than the ability to have a conversation or tell others what to do. Communication is not just about talking *at* other people; it involves active listening to figure out what they are saying. It's about capturing where people are coming from and ensuring that you understand their message before trying to impart yours.

Fortunately, you can develop communication abilities and improve your conflict management skills. Although the topic of managing disputes rationally is often not taught in schools, it's especially critical for project managers whose job is to manage competing demands from a variety of groups with different goals.

On the other hand, perhaps you're having difficulties with your team members delivering the project on time and budget. You're under a lot of unrelenting pressure from stakeholders to meet deadlines or add in extras beyond the initial scope. You may have struggled to get what you wanted from stakeholders. Thus, negotiation is another crucial skill for project managers that you can apply in all other areas of life, and it too can be learned and practiced.

Maybe you feel like you're being accused of things that are well outside your control. As a project manager, you know that you're the one ultimately accountable, yet external issues occur, and not all of them are preventable. Nonetheless, your performance is negatively affected anyway.

These are common issues for project managers. The good news is that not only are there known solutions to these problems, but most of them can be learned and developed with time and experience. Some people may innately seem able to find the solutions on their own, but for the rest of us, practice and dedication to improving will get us there.

In even better news, *the solutions you need are in this book*. You'll learn practical steps for tackling the issues you're facing and effective ways to improve your game. Becoming a mature project manager by developing your leadership abilities has obvious benefits for you personally. You'll no longer be feeling like you're rolling a heavy boulder up a steep hill because, once you can apply these solutions, you'll find your work has become fun, engaging, and rewarding again.

As a project manager *rock star*, you'll have the pick of opportunities because everyone wants to work with a PM that gets things done

and plays well with others. Not only will lucrative clients want to hire you, but star team members will want to be part of your team. You'll feel less pressure and stress. Part of being a great leader is the ability to find win-win solutions that may not be obvious at first glance. Once you develop your talent for this, you'll discover whole new worlds opening up for your dream career.

You probably already know that *leadership* isn't only about the leader; it takes into account their followers too. There are benefits to others when you have developed yourself into a true leader. Stakeholders will find their expectations met or exceeded and the project delivered on time and budget. Also, developing the talents of those who work for you will help them level up their own skills and feel confident in taking on new challenges and responsibilities.

At this point, you may be wondering what qualifies me to provide all this information about the leadership in project management. I've been a project manager myself, for many different companies, and on various projects—from small to large and simple to complex. As I developed my skills, I discovered that the next level up was in improving my leadership skills. I've seen many leaders—both PMs and otherwise—succeed and fail, and I've captured those lessons for you.

I want to help PMs at any stage in their careers level up and become leaders, not just managers. The more leaders the profession has, the better off our clients and we will be. I'm sharing my knowledge in this book, so you can learn from past experiences and become the best project leader that you can be. Everyone has enormous leadership potential within themselves, including you.

In this book, we'll discuss what leadership looks like in the modern world and the critical nature of interpersonal relationships. You'll learn how to improve your problem-solving skills—including leveraging politics—to make your projects better. You will also discover how to manage conflicts and the necessary step to build and manage a successful project team.

You'll also learn how to develop your team members personally and delegate tasks to them without hesitation. This book contains excellent tips on how to achieve more from negotiations and facilitate productive meetings. As a bonus, I introduce the idea of servant leadership, with emphasis on listening, empathy, and emotional intelligence.

You'll discover better ways to deal with stakeholders, set expectations, and use your influence and persuasion powers. In the last chapter, we will uncover four critical capabilities hidden behind the abbreviation of HECG, which are game changers in today's world.

Does this sound great? I am sure you have developed certain technical skills and leadership capabilities during your career. But maybe you feel like you're missing something, or perhaps the fun has disappeared out of a job? Why wait to turn that around and lose this opportunity?

If you want to become a unique project leader, go ahead and get started on this book. *Become the leader of your dreams!*

CHAPTER 1

INTRODUCTION TO LEADERSHIP

YOU'VE probably heard and read a lot about leadership, especially if you're already a project manager (PM). What does it mean exactly, and how does it translate to being a PM? In the first book of this bundle, we discussed the difference between a "manager" and a "leader." Managers focus on the tactical aspects of the project; leaders focus on the strategic.

Although your title is project manager, you are a *project leader* too. The more you can develop your authority as a project leader, the more capable you'll be of implementing complex projects, and the more people will want to work with you.

Leadership in a Nutshell

Leadership is a combination of skills, characteristics, and behaviors. Everyone has a distinct style. The good news is that wherever you perceive your leadership abilities to be right now, you can develop them further through training, good coaching and role models, and the desire to improve continuously.

As a PM, you have to master several technical skills, such as managing the scope of a project. You need to budget appropriately and communicate well with your team and stakeholders. Building relationships at all levels of the client's management hierarchy is necessary to generate a win. You should have a good knowledge of the tasks required to successfully complete the project and develop a schedule that doesn't tax your resources unnecessarily while still satisfying the client.

In addition—and probably most importantly—you must be able to lead your team and not just manage it. You need to influence your team members to do their jobs to the best of their abilities. You'll need to develop some leadership capabilities in addition to your technical skills that will make you a sought-after PM.

Project Manager as CEO

When thinking about project leadership, consider yourself the Chief Executive Officer (CEO) of your project. You're the one who would be ultimately accountable for its success, just as the CEO is responsible when the business starts going in the wrong direction.

The CEO sets the vision and direction for the business. They aren't the ones organizing employee schedules and assigning tasks. Similarly—and especially when you're working on agile projects—you will let the team members figure out how to get the work done according to schedule and leverage each member's strengths for the better.

Successful CEOs differ from their less successful counterparts in nine key areas of leadership capability (Stamoulis, n.d.)[1] These areas fit the strengths that a project manager needs to command a successful project.

1. Taking calculated risks

Playing it safe won't allow you or your team to grow. On the other hand, great leaders don't take unnecessary risks or act carelessly.

As a project manager, you must make decisions with imperfect information. However, you have to take the time to gather enough data and consider the consequences before moving forward.

2. Thinking ahead

CEOs are often compared to being a ship's captain. Poor managers and team members tend to focus on what's right in front of them. Imagine how quickly you'd run into trouble if you were only viewing the sea right in front of you.

Instead, looking far ahead will help you spot the icebergs early, so you can have time to steer around them. You must be the one scanning the horizon to spot those icebergs.

3. Thoughtful bias toward action

People who ruminate or analyze carefully are often helpful to the team. However, the executive needs to be focused on the actions to take.

Good leaders aren't taking action just to do something; they're taking action based on a thoughtful reason. If there's a rationale for the action, they will take it.

4. Optimistic

Henry Ford said, "Whether you think you can, or you think you can't, you're right." To stay optimistic and keep the team motivated, the leader must believe that the task can be done. They must also be the lookout for new opportunities and pursue them when it makes sense to do so.

5. Tough and tender

An old saying specific to project management is that if everyone's angry with you, you've done your job. You can't please everyone, so don't waste your time trying. A great leader will make unpopular decisions because they're looking ahead where the others aren't. They've spotted new opportunities, which means that people will need to change something, though most people don't like change.

A thick skin is necessary for your leadership as a PM, so you can let these comments roll off your back. You keep going, even after your team members have expressed their displeasure.

At the same time, you're not insensitive. Great executives don't just demand a change of their workers but help them adjust. They acknowledge when people are having a difficult time and don't seek to enforce their ideas through power or coercion. Instead, they influence and persuade. Finally, they distinguish between resistance to change and valid arguments and promote team members who come with better ideas than their own.

6. Emotional intelligence (EQ)

Later in the book, we'll go into more detail about EQ for leaders. For now, it's essential to know that top CEOs understand and can manage their emotions effectively. They display their feelings and don't bottle them up. At the same time, they don't allow their emotions to overwhelm their reason or affect their team negatively.

7. Ability to read people well

Being able to read people means that you have developed emotional intelligence. As a leader, you want to understand the various perspectives that people from different backgrounds bring to their work and how to combine and support them optimally.

8. Pragmatically inclusive

As a PM, you already know that you don't know everything, and that other people's viewpoints can be extremely valuable. You will need to make many decisions, and the smart thing to do will be to get feedback from other people.

However, you still need to make the decision yourself. Just because most people you speak to think that option A is correct, they could still be wrong. If you are sure that option B is right, you need to choose it, even though you're alone in your opinion.

9. Trusting within reason

CEOs need to be comfortable with a variety of people with a wide range of backgrounds and experiences. As a project manager, your team will include members with various experiences and skills.

"Trust, but verify." —Russian proverb[2]

You will often be in a position to hire your team members, and if you've worked with them before, you will probably have a higher level of trust in them. On the other hand, just like a CEO, you cannot trust everyone you work with blindly.

The Changing Face of Leadership

You might have noticed that many of the preceding leadership skills are interpersonal. Today's CEOs don't throw their weight around the way they may have done so back in the last century. Now, when business leaders misbehave, they're often frowned upon by the wider community.

Today's leaders have discovered the power of emotional intelligence (EQ) in their work. Unlike IQ, which has standardized tests and measures cognitive thought, EQ is the measure of interpersonal intelligence. There are three basic EQ skills involved (Psychology Today, n.d.)[3]:

1. Recognize your own emotions (self-awareness)
2. Manage the emotions (self-regulation)
3. Help others to manage their emotions (social awareness)

Fortunately, unlike IQ, which is largely fixed, there are ways to develop your EQ. You don't have to practice these tips at work only, but in your personal life as well.

- **Practice naming your emotions**

    For those who are already tuned into their feelings, this tip may not be as difficult as it is for other people. When you recognize that you just don't feel quite right, try to name the emotion you're having. Boredom? Frustration? Anger? Irritation? Be as specific as you can.

    Also, try to note what the trigger was. Were you in a situation where you didn't feel like you were in control? Was there feedback you didn't want to hear?

- **Ask what others think about your EQ**

    Speaking of something you may not want to hear, ask friends, family, and colleagues for their impression of your emotional intelligence. Where do they think you're lacking? Remember not to shoot the messenger—you need them to be honest, so you can identify the spots you want to improve.

- **Read novels**

    Sometimes people in business read only nonfiction if they read at all. They will often read biographies of successful people, inspirational material to stay motivated, or educational books. Nonfiction is important, but add in some novels and fictional literature.

    They allow you to literally step into someone else's shoes and live their life. It's a great way to develop the empathy you need to be an emotionally intelligent leader.

- **Manage stress**

    This skill is vital for all project managers, and not just the ones seeking to increase their EQ! PMs must juggle many tasks and concepts themselves while handling team members and stakeholders. It can be exhausting and lead to burnout. It also makes you irritable and less likely to communicate in an emotionally intelligent way with others.

    You probably know the basics already: enough sleep, nutritious food, exercise, and mindfulness practices.

    If you have a hard time sleeping, make sure your room is cool and dark, and shut down screens well before going to bed; not five minutes—more like an hour, so the blue light emitted doesn't interfere with your circadian rhythm. You can use that time to read your novel and help you be more empathetic.

    Were you having a tough time with exercise? Maybe your daily "stand-up" meeting should be a daily "walking" meeting instead, especially if you and the team can get outside to do it. Don't skip this vital step of getting your body in motion because it does increase your productivity and boosts your mood.

Leader as Visionary

One of the most critical roles that a commander has is being a visionary. CEOs create the vision so the entire crew can be on board and everyone can work to achieve the same mission—all row in the same direction. The captain sets the course by which the ship will sail.

Yet, there's more to successfully reaching the destination than just having the vision. The captain has to motivate the crew to do their best and keep rowing in the right direction. To maximize resources in terms of human capital, the captain needs to understand what drives them.

Also, the captain is the one who would coach the crew. Ship captains typically started as crew members, just as many project managers started out belowdecks as team members. Therefore, they're in the perfect position to work with individual members on improving their craft and skills. If the crew members don't know how to do their job properly, the ship won't reach its destination. Highly qualified crew members want to improve themselves, and good captains know that the more skills the crew has, the more likely they will be to succeed.

To achieve their goal, the captain must also ensure that the crew has the resources it needs. On a more grand ship, like a Viking ship or frigate, they would need oars, food, time off, and sleeping quarters, among other things.

On land in a project, team members need slightly different resources, but the PM must still ensure they have what they need in terms of materials and resources. Some projects might get by with a whiteboard and enough laptops for everyone; whereas others may require more. The project manager won't usually be the one going out to the office supply store to pick up some dry erase markers, but they would ensure the job gets done.

Captains are also responsible for problem solving on a higher level. Later in the book, we'll delve into this topic more deeply. Fundamentally, the captain's vision should not only set the course, but also look ahead for potential icebergs or other obstacles that could impede the ship's safe passage. When such problems are encountered, the captain has to figure out how to deal with them.

Likewise, the project manager must be on the lookout for hurdles that could block the team's progress and determine how to avoid or mitigate them. Problems could arise from communication issues with the client, natural disasters, or other external issues. To ensure that the team can complete the project successfully, the PM must clear away any obstacles or plan to move around them.

To win, they must be proactive. Captains don't wait until the ship is a few yards away from an iceberg to plot the course around it. Similarly, when a hurdle appears on a project, the project manager needs to solve the problem sooner rather than later, instead of allowing the molehill to grow to a mountain's size. Recall that great leaders are biased toward action.

Interpersonal Capabilities

Communicating, coaching, and dealing with stakeholders and clients—a project manager needs to possess excellent interpersonal skills to deliver successful projects consistently. There are a handful of abilities that PMs should stay on top of.

- **Communication (verbal and nonverbal)**

    Studies have found that most of a speaker's message is not in the words that they use, but in their voice and body language (Nguyen, 2014).[4] Although it's obviously essential to get the words right, it's even more critical to make sure that your tone of voice, speed of speech, and body language are supporting what you want to say—not working against it.

Imagine that you are speaking to someone who is standing in front of you with their head down and arms crossed over their chest. After you're done, in monotone, they tell you that they really enjoyed what you had to say. Would you believe them? Of course not: they seem defensive and disinterested.

Positive body language is constructive. When you're standing up talking to someone, make sure you point your body toward them, including your feet. Make eye contact, though be careful not to be creepy or appear too intense. Stay relaxed with your hands at your sides without fidgeting; however, you may use hand gestures to support your points.

- **Active listening**

Have you ever been talking to someone, and the instant you take a breath, they jump in, and it's obvious they were just waiting for you to finish so they could make their point? Or maybe you were the one nodding your head impatiently and hoping the other would hurry up and finish so you could speak.

By contrast, active listening is when you absorb what the speaker is saying thoroughly, retain it, and respond appropriately. This would require you to pay attention to what they're saying—not what their speech sparks in you or the funny anecdote you have about a similar situation. Also, you shouldn't judge nor dismiss what they're saying. What they're talking about may be new or strange to you, making it even more crucial that you not judge, so you can truly understand their message.

You may want to repeat back some of what you heard to clarify or summarize what you got from their speech. This shows the other person that you were listening to and understand exactly what they're saying. Likewise, it could voice how you don't, and they can explain it again.

Active listening helps ensure there are no misunderstandings or miscommunication. It also puts people at ease and shows that their needs are important too. This often becomes essential when you're de-escalating conflict, as we'll get into later in the book.

- **Assertiveness**

Sometimes people confuse assertiveness with aggressiveness, but they are different attitudes.

Aggressive people run roughshod over others. Such a manager would be more likely to tell their followers what to do while not allowing any questions or concerns to surface.

By contrast, a commander needs to be *assertive*. These leaders are direct and honest about what they want. They stand up for themselves, but without making other people feel bullied or disrespected. They're not accusing other people of doing something wrong, and they often use "I" statements.

For example, rather than telling a client, "You didn't get me the materials I requested," they might say something like, "I haven't yet received the materials. Do you know when I can expect them to be delivered?"

- **Self-confidence**

To advocate for yourself and your team members, you need to trust in your abilities and judgment while believing that you are worthy. If you have a lot of self-doubts or are too self-critical, you won't be able to make the hard decisions required of a *successful* project manager. You have to be able to think independently, which means that you have confidence in your thoughts even when others seem to be thinking differently.

When you're self-confident, you're able to admit to your own mistakes, because you know that being human doesn't make you a bad person. This allows other people to bond with you because you're not pretending to be perfect.

You're more willing to take calculated risks when you're confident in your decision-making. You know that you've weighed the pros and cons and can make a choice, even with imperfect information.

People want to (literally) follow the leader. They don't want to follow someone who acts like they don't know what they're doing, or appear nervous or unsure. This is why so many con men are successful—such people act confidently, and others are taken in.

As a project manager, creating an atmosphere of confidence encourages not only your team but also the client. They don't want to hand over the reins on something that could cost thousands—if not millions—of dollars to someone who doesn't know what they're doing.

Upgrade Your Interpersonal Behavior

How do you think you rate on the previous skills? Are there areas where you believe you need to improve? Fortunately, just as you can improve your EQ (which is the foundation of interpersonal skills), you can also get better with your interpersonal capabilities. Most of these can be practiced at home and in business. You'll have ample opportunity to become better at building relationships, which is critical to success as a leader.

- **Act with personal integrity**

    Stand up for what you believe in and question when others ask you to do something that goes against the company's or your core

values. Whether you're at home or work, make sure you're aligned with what's important to you. Others will see that you stick to your principles and deliver what you promise, and they can build their trust in you.

- **Manage agreement**

  Managing conflict is a crucial component in leading a successful project, so I've devoted a chapter to it later. However, I'm mentioning it here because managing agreement is vital for interpersonal skills. Here, you would help people build trust and learn to collaborate. Providing constructive feedback will help maintain the agreement while allowing you to deal with difficult situations before they grow into mountains.

  You can practice this by looking for agreements whenever you're talking to other people, especially during conversations where views differ.

- **Reduce or remove distractions**

  It's hard to listen actively to others when your phone vibrates and buzzes with social media or email notifications. Turn them off, or, better yet, disable them entirely. Put your phone face down on a nearby table or counter, so you can't see your screen. Doing all this will help you pay attention to the person you're listening to.

- **Allow silence to happen**

  Some people are uncomfortable with silence and will rush to fill it with words. However, sometimes, not talking is the appropriate response if you've been listening because you may need time to put your thoughts in order. You don't have to babble while you do so; silence doesn't have to be bad, so let it happen when it fits.

- **Don't make others feel accused or wrong**

    When you're standing up for yourself, it's important not to do so by putting others down. Practice using "I" statements and not accusing others with "You didn't," "You should have," or any other kinds of blaming or accusation statements.

    If there are issues with other people, you cannot ignore them because that's how molehills grow. You can discuss them and stand up for yourself by being direct and explaining what you need.

    Obviously, this one works well at home too. Stop accusing your spouse or children and see how much more cooperative they become. Practicing this type of assertiveness will serve you well in all aspects of life.

- **Set boundaries**

    Just as you must ask for what you need, it's important to set boundaries, so people know when they're overstepping. Enforce them too, so others aren't demanding too much of your time and energy.

    I had a boss that would try to get the most out of his employees for what he paid us. You could end up working all night to finish something under his leadership. But I discovered that he was perfectly fine with boundaries. If you told him that you needed to go home to spend time with your pets/kids/spouse and work on it the next day, he was okay with that.

    I don't think he meant it maliciously; I just had to let him know that he couldn't expect me to work late every night when I could get things done on time. There were times when I did need to work late to finish, and I didn't resent it thanks to the boundaries I had set.

- **Fake it 'til you make it**

    This approach does not work for project managers most of the time! You truly do need to have excellent technical and leadership skills to lead projects successfully. However, there is one area where it does work, and that's in *self-confidence*. The more you act confidently (even if you aren't so at that moment), the more confident you will be. The more confident you are, the more you'll act confidently, and so on in a positive upward spiral.

    Another benefit of being self-confident is that you will be more comfortable taking risks. The more you choose, the more confident you'll be about taking the next one, and so on.

    How can you fake being confident? Start with how you stand and deliver when you're talking to other people. Smiling shows confidence, as does looking people in the eyes and standing up strong and tall. Fidgeting, looking away, mumbling, talking fast, and facing away from the person you're talking to all signal a lack of confidence.

    Also, dress well, especially when you're networking or speaking in front of an audience. Make sure everything fits and is clean with nothing that needs mending. Fiddling with loose buttons or threads will not make you appear confident.

    You can use power poses to help psych yourself up (just not in front of other people, as noted in the section about being assertive above.) Again, stand straight but not rigid; plant your feet wider than shoulder-width apart; and stand with your hands on your hips in a Superman pose for a few minutes.

- **Work on self-confidence**

    There are other ways to build up your confidence besides faking it. When you know, you'll be facing something difficult—like an interview or an annual review with your supervisor—prepare ahead of time and do your homework.

When you're dealing with people you don't know, look them up beforehand on LinkedIn, as well as the company. Gather any intelligence you can on other social media sites and decide how you can be of service to them. What problems do they face? Be an expert on them when you eventually meet them.

Employers will ask plenty of general questions during interviews, such as "Where do you think you'll be five years from now?" or "Give me an example of a problem that you solved in the past." Have answers to these questions ready when you walk through the door.

Otherwise, you may need to prepare some facts for your boss, such as all the money you've saved the company with your productivity system or testimonials from clients who are pleased with your work. If you know you made mistakes, and your boss will bring them up, prepare what you'll say so you can respond calmly and logically. Show how you learned from that error.

For any situation, create and maintain a list of your accomplishments. Everything counts, even the small ones. Sometimes, the small wins are what will keep you going until you can achieve a bigger result. Before you go into a situation that will likely make you tense or feel less than confident, study your list. Remind yourself of what you have done rather than focusing on what you haven't.

Key Takeaways

Successful project managers are leaders and develop leadership, interpersonal, and communication skills.

- There are specific capabilities that strong leaders have, such as a bias toward action and being independent decision makers who ask for others' opinions when appropriate.

- Modern leaders develop their emotional intelligence, so they can inspire and motivate their team.

- As a project manager, you're responsible for setting the vision for everyone and coaching your team to work their best to achieve the goal.

- Interpersonal capabilities are crucial for PMs, and those who feel lacking in some areas can work on them to improve.

In the next chapter, you will learn how to deal with politics and problems.

---

[1] https://www.russellreynolds.com/insights/thought-leadership/making-it-to-the-top-nine-attributes-that-differentiate-ceos
[2] https://en.wikipedia.org/wiki/Trust,_but_verify
[3] https://www.psychologytoday.com/us/basics/emotional-intelligence
[4] https://www.entrepreneur.com/article/239831

CHAPTER 2

GOT A PROBLEM?

CRITICAL skills required for leaders include solving problems. You know Murphy's Law: if something can go wrong, it will! This is especially true for projects because they are complex in many aspects. Although your team members should have the knowledge and authority to deal with smaller issues that pop up from time to time, you're responsible for handling the big, tough ones. Not only do you need to solve them, but you must do so quickly and effectively, so the team can get back to focusing on finishing their tasks as soon as possible.

Problems in Projects

Sometimes, you'll be dealing with relatively small and insignificant problems, though you should mostly leave them to your team.

However, you should pay attention to the bigger ones that would be beyond your team's capabilities or require your bird's-eye view to solve. On the other hand, sometimes you need to kick away the small pebbles, just so your team can have a smooth surface to travel on.

Here are some of the major challenges that project teams may face.

- **Insufficient resources**

    No one wants to throw away good money when a problem arises. But sometimes the answer really *is* to provide more money, people, or time to take care of it.

    The way to preempt this type of problem is to plan the resource allocation better. Know upfront how much you need to complete the project successfully. If it will take two teams of six people each, then budget for twelve people—not just ten or eleven to make the budget "look" better. During planning, overestimate the required resources to account for any unforeseen issues.

    If it's a project you haven't led before or tasks you're not familiar with, ask. The client themselves may have completed a similar project, or someone else on your team has. Get their input and review case studies. Like the Boy Scouts, be prepared.

- **Poor planning**

    This problem falls squarely on your shoulders as the project manager. You are ultimately responsible for the planning and execution of the project. If you don't plan correctly, even a flawless execution will not allow you to reach your goal.

    Know how to prioritize, break down the work into manageable and measurable tasks, and estimate the time and resources involved.

Again, if you haven't worked with a project like that before, ask for help and find experts who know how to steer you in the right direction.

- **Gap in leadership**

    Lack of leadership will hurt you at the client level, and sometimes it's a result of a gap in your own skills. If the project sponsor or key manager with the client isn't an effective leader, you may find it more challenging to secure a win.

    By the same token, if you need to work on your leadership skills, get going on those *yesterday!* You probably won't be natural in many aspects, but practice and improve. Remember that you don't just have to exercise these abilities at work—you can also find ways to develop them at home or school. We will cover many essential leadership skills within this book.

- **Personnel issues**

    When people work together, there will be conflicts. Some left unresolved will almost certainly torpedo your chances of success. We'll discuss managing conflict in the next chapter. In the meantime, just make sure to encourage members to work together and with the stakeholders.

    You can set a good example by using your listening and communication skills to deal healthily with people who disagree with your tactics, are unmotivated, or have other issues. Model these capabilities for all others involved in the project.

- **Vague requirements**

    It's tough to deliver a project successfully when you don't know what success means, or when they change abruptly and halfway through the process. Make the requirements clear and measurable from the start and document them. If the client continues to provide vague answers, you need to repeat the parameters until you get the ones you can use.

If someone requests a change, make sure you have written into the plan that you must approve it before moving forward. That way, you can prevent the project from drifting and scope creep.

- **Stakeholder issues**

    Sometimes, the stakeholders aren't sure or clear about what they want, or you may have missed a critical constituency that shows up when you're almost finished. In response, the stakeholders may complain that they can't use the result. They may want to increase the scope without providing additional resources or be disinterested in the project's success and not helpful when you need their input.

    Identifying everyone involved and letting them know what's in it for them will be crucial to your success. Communicating effectively with all stakeholders and getting them involved is critical, so you'll need strong stakeholder management skills as a PM.

There are also smaller issues that you'll need to deal with along the way. Most projects have several moving parts, each with its own deadline. For example, the project may involve two devices, and you're not sure how they connect. You would develop a prototype for the connecting bit and test it. Until you've resolved that issue, you will be unable to move forward.

Steps for Solving Problems

There's a basic 5-step framework for doing so. As always, the devil is in the details.

1. Characterize the problem accurately

Before you can solve the problem, you need to define it precisely. If you end up trying to solve the symptoms rather than the disease, you'll take longer because whatever fix you decide on won't take care of the issue.

Suppose the client complains about one of your team members. Is the problem that the team member is a poor worker, or that their communication skills need some work? Were the client's expectations set too high? You can see that the solutions you come up with will differ, depending on how you diagnose the problem.

2. Determine the root cause

There will be times when the cause will be apparent, though you should still perform some analysis to ensure that you're not missing or omitting anything. In other cases, you'll need to dig more. The first cause that you stumble upon may not be the true reason, so you need to work to find the root and ensure that the problem doesn't recur in the future.

- **Fishbone diagram**

    This type of diagram (also called the *cause and effect* or *Ishikawa* diagram) helps teams figure out the main cause of a problem. The problem is stated and a line drawn horizontally next to it, which forms the "spine" of the fish.

    Next, the team determines the main categories of the potential causes of the problem. Each category is drawn on a diagonal line to the spine with some above and some below. They typically include Method, Machines, People, Environment, Materials, and Measurement (ASQ, n.d.)[5]

    Now the team can brainstorm possible causes of the problem for each category.

- *Flowchart*

    This may be particularly helpful when your problem relates to a specific process or workflow. Use or create a flowchart of how the work proceeds along its path, then identify the choke points where the process gets held up. This type of visual aid is great for linear thinkers.

- *Five Whys*

    A popular root cause analysis framework is the Five Whys (Wikipedia, 2020).[6] You would ask why the problem occurred, and when you get an answer, ask why the answer happened, and continue going deeper. You may only need to ask why three times, or you may need to ask more than five times. However, if you keep asking, you'll eventually get to the root.

    Suppose you decided that the client's complaint referred to the team worker's communication skills. Why did they send an email that offended the client? Because they were trying to lighten the mood and missed the mark. Why were they trying to lighten the mood? They were worried that the client would be upset because the deliverable would be delayed a week. Why is the deliverable being delayed a week? Because the critical material was not ordered on time. Why wasn't the order made on time? Because no one knew the material would be needed upfront. Why did no one know? Because the project was new to everyone on the team.

    And there you have it. The root cause of the client's complaint was essentially poor planning upfront!

You want to check that the cause is likely to be the culprit. Does it explain all the phenomena you've seen related to the problem? Depending on what it is, you can probably run a test to confirm that such is the root cause. Take that opportunity when you can, so you don't end up solving the wrong problem and have to go through the process again later.

3. Brainstorm or mind-map solutions

Here's where you and the team would get creative. Make sure the atmosphere for any brainstorming or mind-mapping sessions is open and inclusive. No idea is stupid, though the team may decide later that it's unworkable. Get all the ideas into the open before you start winnowing down.

Finding potential solutions in a group is more valuable than one person doing it alone. For one thing, more minds would generate more ideas. If your team is diverse enough and with different backgrounds, it should be coming up with various ideas.

Brainstorming works best when no one feels ashamed or unworthy. Someone may come up with an idea that isn't quite what the team was looking for, but others could find that it sparks another idea, and that would be how you find creative answers that work.

4. Pick the optimal one

With a functional, creative team, you might well end up with several solutions that work. As the project manager, you should be aware of the project's priorities in terms of timeframe, cost, and quality.

As you could see in the first book of this bundle, you can pick two of the three: fast, cheap, or good. Which solution maximizes the priority? If there's more than one, which of them optimizes for your second priority?

5. Execute

Going through the problem-solving process is great, but you cannot actually solve it until you implement the answer you found in step 4. Do so decisively and move on. If you're waffling about implementing the solution, you may need to go back to the previous step and confirm that you've chosen the right solution.

Complex Projects

The five-step model above is a pretty simple framework. Often, when you're working on a project, there will be added complexities or other considerations to take into account.

- **The interrelatedness of systems and machines**

    In the old days, it might have been a simple matter to isolate the cause of a malfunction and repair it. Machine #4 had grit in the gears, so it was fixed quickly with cleaning and some lubricant.

    Today, however, most systems are interrelated. Machines are often guided by software, and when something breaks down, you may need to call in the IT department instead of a mechanic.

    Such makes problem solving more complicated. You need to consider all systems involved with a specific machine as potential causes, and isolating the variables can be tricky.

- **No quick fixes for long-term problems**

    The bias toward action and urgency that many people feel when an issue arises may lead to poor problem solving. You could create a Band-Aid for the problem, but how long will it last? Will you be merely delaying a long-term fix in favor of repeating a short-term one? At what point does that become more costly than taking a bit longer to implement a repair that will solve the issue over the long run?

    Eliminating possible causes makes it easier to conduct the root-cause analysis and will prevent you from trying to solve the wrong problem. In fact, according to one PMI conference paper, the first objective should not be to solve the problem but to avoid doing something stupid (Morfin, 2000).[7]

- **Who needs to be involved**

    Teams that believe they're under pressure to solve the problem quickly might try to answer the problem themselves, assuming that it will be faster. However, it may not be the optimal answer.

    Consider the stakeholders involved. If they object to the solution that your team devises, you'll have lost a lot of time. In some cases, stakeholders need to be involved in one or more intermediate steps of the process: data gathering, brainstorming, and choosing the optimal solution.

    This is particularly true if you're having difficulty choosing between two strong options—the stakeholders can help you by expressing their priorities. Don't hinder your problem-solving process by ignoring valuable input from others.

- **Specify the problem**

    Be precise about the problem. For example, "Productivity is too low" is vague, and your team members may object strenuously to that kind of summary of the problem. "The widget production is a week behind schedule" is a specific way to state what's happening and avoid presupposing blame.

    A great way to gather information is to ask "is/is not" questions, allowing you to eliminate potential causes more quickly. For example, where is the issue happening, and where is the issue *not* happening? If widget production on Assembly Line A is a week behind but right on time on Line B, you can focus on Line A to identify the cause.

    When does it happen and when does it *not* happen? Widget production falls behind when Machine 1 is down, but not when Machine 2 is down.

    Give it some parameters. How big is the problem? How big could it be?

- **Data overload**

    We've talked about the necessity of making decisions based on imperfect data. In the modern world, everyone is drowning in data. This makes solutions more difficult because first you have to figure out what is related and relevant to the problem. Most information will probably be nothing more than a *distraction*.

    Relevant information will be precise about the problem and support the goal directly. It's must-have information, whereas much of what you'll see is only nice to have.

- **Avoid analysis paralysis**

    Directly related to data overload, many modern teams find it all too easy to lapse into spending too long on the analysis. Throw out data that isn't relevant and only useful in distracting from the main problem. Sticking with your list of data-gathering questions will help you and the team to avoid collecting unnecessary information. Avoid delaying the last few steps of the process when you don't have to.

    Spending too much time in the analysis is a form of procrastination. If you and the team are not confident in your problem-solving abilities, this may prevent you from taking the steps necessary to implement a solution.

Politics

Whenever you have people, you'll have politics. Don't pretend that the issue doesn't exist, ignore it, or work around it as if it will just go away. To complete the project successfully, you'll need to ensure that interpersonal issues are resolved.

Identifying likely allies and skeptics upfront will help you tailor the message specifically to them. The more influential people you have

on your side, the better. You can enlist their help in dealing with those who are unsure of or actively opposing the project. Finding influencers isn't always easy because you cannot use titles as proxies. There may be someone who is listened to by many in the organization while having little to no executive authority. Determining ahead of time who is ready and willing to champion you and the project will get you closer to success.

What distractions pull time and attention away from your project or might affect your champions? Understanding all active forces in the organization is helpful as well. Be aware of other projects that are happening concurrently.

Also, try to discover whether the company had embarked on similar change efforts before you got there. What were the results? If a previous project failed, you must understand the factors and that some skepticism about the projects' wisdom has probably infected much of the staff.

Your team's performance is important too. When they're doing well, make sure you communicate that, especially to the project sponsor and any other project champions you identified. When they're not, it's up to you to figure out how to get them back on track. Do they need more resources? Coaching? Communication with stakeholders is similarly crucial. You can transmit your excitement and keep them interested and engaged in its success.

In addition to politics, when there are people, there will be conflict. We'll discuss how to handle it healthily in the next chapter. In fact, healthy conflict can drive better solutions for problems because you're listening to different viewpoints.

You and your team can use politics positively to help you influence others. Seen another way, you're building and developing a network that can help you and your team succeed.

- **Create a good impression**

    Make sure the important people find you knowledgeable and approachable. They may be senior management or influencers within the department. You don't have to bend over backward, but it would be a good idea to pay them special attention.

- **Nurture mentor opportunities**

    A fundamental characteristic in most people is the desire to help others. People to whom you go for counsel feel important and worthy when you ask them for their advice and feedback. They can become strong allies for your cause as well.

- **Be in the right place at the right time**

    Position yourself to take advantage of opportunities when they come your way.

- **Be strategic in your appointments**

    Make sure that you're taking the time to visit senior executives, management, stakeholders, and influencers. Let them know about you and your team's accomplishments and progress.

    Communicate when there's a way that you can help them personally. They may or may not take you up on it, but the mere offer is powerful. Managers and leaders notice proactive people and prefer them.

- **Build your "favor bank"**

    Favors are usually thought of as reciprocal: you scratch my back; I'll scratch yours. By doing things for others, even or especially when they don't benefit you directly, you're building up favors. When you need one, you'll have plenty of people to ask.

Politics can also be used negatively. Avoid the following because you'll be seen as less of a leader when engaging in these unconstructive behaviors. Remember that trust is built over a long time, but it can be lost very quickly. If you want a good reputation, then avoid the following in all situations.

- **Feinting**

    If you pretend to be interested in one alternative but are using the pretense to take another maneuver, you're destroying the trust that people may otherwise have had in you. A similar situation would be allowing someone to believe that the project is in one condition when, in reality, it's another.

- **Deceiving**

    You already know that honesty—including emotional honesty—is a crucial concept for any leader. Lying for any reason shows a fake facade.

- **Entrapping**

    Manipulating anyone into a bad position where they could lose face, a promotion, or even a job is something that no good project manager would ever stoop to doing. Whether you like or dislike someone is irrelevant.

    It may seem in the short term that getting rid of someone who opposes the project will increase its chances of success. However, that's an illusion. There may be more than one person who's skeptical of the project, so removing one obstacle won't solve the problem.

- **Backbiting**

    Making up negative information or curating a story to show someone in a bad light is another maneuver doomed to fail, and it will hurt your reputation. Good leaders are guided by their values; they don't allow short-term calculations to ruin their long-term opportunities for success.

Does it seem like politics and leadership are two completely separate concepts or ends of a spectrum? When used appropriately, politics can be an essential part of leadership. No one can do everything alone, including the completion of a successful project. As a PM, you'll need to rely on others to support you and help you carry the message. Politics—or using your powers of influence and persuasion—is nothing more than a way to build up your group of allies.

It will assist you in keeping your project on track, and you can then avoid potential political landmines. Knowing where they all are at the beginning is helpful in this regard. Understanding how to use your influence constructively will also help you shield your team from negative political consequences, so everyone can stay focused.

Key Takeaways

Problems and politics occur on every project, and a successful project manager acknowledges them to resolve issues effectively.

- A few common problems tend to crop up in projects, including stakeholder and personnel issues, vague requirements, and insufficient planning.

- A five-step model in solving problems is useful as a framework for any issue that arises.

- Particular attention must be paid to finding the root cause of the problem to ensure that your solution will completely fix the issue, and you won't have to revisit it later.

- Politics can be used either constructively or destructively. When you use your powers of influence for good, you increase your chances of success significantly.

In the next chapter, you will learn how to manage and appreciate conflict.

---

[5] https://**asq.org**/quality-resources/fishbone
[6] https://**en.wikipedia.org**/wiki/Five_whys
[7] https://**www.pmi.org**/learning/library/appraisal-situation-problem-solving-projects-492

CHAPTER 3

FIGHT! LEARN TO LOVE THE CONFLICT YOU'RE IN

CONFLICT is a feature—not a bug when done right. It means that you have a diverse group of people with different backgrounds and opinions. A hive mind, where everyone thinks alike and has essentially the same experience, doesn't have conflict. It also does not produce innovative or optimal solutions to the problems it faces. Leadership requires you to encourage the expression of healthy conflict and eliminate or reduce destructive conflict.

Inevitable Conflict

Just as problems and politics always arise when you have more than one person in a room, so too does disagreement. Ignoring the discord doesn't mean it's not there. In fact, it may even be more dangerous if it's simmering beneath the surface rather than out in the open. Unresolved conflict doesn't go away, and it often boils over just when things are at their worst.

Particularly with more diverse teams, the human brain works against collaboration because it has a tendency to divide the world into *Us vs. Them*, and anyone who isn't clearly *Us* must, by definition, be *Them*. The brain has two systems that balance trusting others and preparing for an attack.

Our old friend, the *amygdala*—where the fight-or-flight reaction resides—is key in distrusting something that might be harmful, like a predator. Remember that on the savannah, humans were in danger of being killed by other animals, unlike in the modern world. We still have that instinct, as we've discussed in the first book of this budle.

On the other hand, we also have the mesolimbic system that provides rewards and pleasure for things that will help the brain flourish and survive. This system releases "happy" neurochemicals, such as dopamine and oxytocin, known to promote bonding between people. Our brains are tilted a bit more toward distrusting new people than bonding, yet that can be overcome with good leadership (Henderson, 2018).[8]

Another cause of conflicts between people has ironically increased with the adoption of agile methodology and its reliance on self-organizing teams. Disagreements escalate when people's roles become ambiguous or poorly defined (Villax et al., 2010).[9]

When there's a clear hierarchy and everyone knows exactly what they're doing, there's little opportunity for miscommunication about the order of things. However, when most of the team is cross-functional, and they must decide among themselves who is responsible for which tasks, disputes often arise. Everyone's sense of fairness must be satisfied, and all must be perceived to be carrying the load equally.

It's not helpful for the team to disagree and argue with each other constantly. After all, the work needs to get done. There are a handful of leadership skills that the project manager can use to avoid unnecessary conflict, which is the kind that serves no purpose other than to be a distraction.

- **Team building**

    Sometimes, people just don't understand each other. When they don't spend much time together, they're less likely to give each other the benefit of the doubt. They'll only collaborate with those they trust.

    Diverse teams demonstrate the importance of having members spend time together. When they don't know each other, it will be more likely that the *Us vs. Them* dichotomy is activated. However, as they spend time together, discover how much they're actually alike, and find some common ground, the balance starts to tilt the other way toward the social pleasure system.

    The key to team building is that the team must spend time together and away from the pressures of the project and learn how their different styles and ideas complement each other. You'll uncover more details about team building later in the book.

- **Negotiation**

    Project managers must be skilled at finding win-win solutions wherever possible. Being able to identify a solution that would allow all parties to feel they got something they wanted out of the deal helps build a foundation for more collaboration and clear away potential resentment.

    When the PM finds solutions upfront, it becomes easier for the team and stakeholders to work together. We will discuss more about successful negotiation in a later chapter.

- **Problem solving**

    As you know from the previous chapter, spotting issues when they arise is key to managing a situation. If there are any apparent conflicts at the onset of the project, the PM can address and resolve them before they disrupt the work.

On the other hand, there will be times when open conflict is necessary and helpful. Managed properly, it can provide some space for those with differing viewpoints to air and explain their views while helping the team arrive at an optimal solution.

Styles of Conflict Management

Most people naturally fall into one of five categories when faced with conflict (Planisware, 2020).[10] However, that doesn't mean you can't adopt other styles when necessary. You do need to understand your own type and its advantages and disadvantages. If destructive aspects of the situation get in the way of resolving conflicts, you may apply any of the following styles to fix the issue.

1. The Competitor

This type often believes there is a finite amount of resources; therefore, if someone gets more than them, they must, by definition, receive less. They are assertive and may exert power at the expense of others.

Advantages: useful when a decision is urgent and needs to be made quickly.

Disadvantages: may cause resentment among others and forego the opportunity to find a win-win that benefits all sides.

2. The Avoider

As you can probably guess, this person does not want to get involved

in the conflict and will evade it, accept decisions made by default, and delegate decisions that might hurt someone's feelings.

Advantages: when the stakes are low and the context trivial, ignoring the conflict can help the team move on.

Disadvantages: when the stakes are high and nontrivial, pretending conflict doesn't exist can result in a bigger issue down the road.

3. The Accommodator

They're cooperative and will give up their own concerns to satisfy others.

Advantages: when cooperation is needed, this attitude is constructive.

Disadvantages: the Accommodator may end up resenting others, and their concerns may be missing when looking for an optimal solution.

4. The Collaborator

People of this type try to find win-win solutions. They don't back down from their concerns, but they also consider others' needs with respect. They are assertive and inclusive.

Advantages: most likely to resolve conflicts to the satisfaction of all involved.

Disadvantages: none.

5. The Compromiser

As you would expect, this type expects everyone to give up a little something to reach a solution. They give up less than the Accommodator but more than the Competitor.

Advantages: useful when time is tight and no one will budge.

Disadvantages: may miss out on opportunities to find a win-win.

Types of Conflict

Over the years and in terms of project management, conflicts have been viewed differently (Villax et al., 2010).[11] First, the *traditional* view was that it was dangerous and should be avoided, which would have been the manager's viewpoint. Next, the *behavioral* concept suggested that, although conflict should be avoided when possible, it is natural and expected. Although conflict in itself is not healthy, it can be resolved in a way that does not harm.

Finally, the *interactionist* viewpoint believes that conflict should be encouraged up to a certain point because it helps increase performance. Airing different views increases innovation and improvement. It drives the organization to find solutions and, when handled well, improves the firm's creative energy.

However, not all types of conflict are healthy and resolved easily to the satisfaction of all. Some should be avoided or eliminated as best the PM can while allowing healthy conflicts generate benefits. Let's look at the different types of conflicts.

- **Interpersonal**

    This type can easily lead to unhealthy conflict. It can be intense and the damage long-lasting, with emotions running high. Chances of project success with people-focused conflict diminish.

    Fostering a spirit of team harmony and encouraging team building are essential for PMs to avoid interpersonal conflict. Otherwise, the team's effectiveness would be decreased, and the project manager must spend too much time dealing with the fallout.

- **Interface**

    When the team clashes with external forces, such as other stakeholder groups, it can also harm their performance. This conflict is also people-focused and typically occurs when different social groups have contrasting attitudes toward the project, especially when the project is large and involves the community.

PMs can decrease this conflict's likelihood by ensuring they identify and reach out to all stakeholders and communicate with them regularly.

- **Global**

    When the project reaches across the world, it's known as global. Culture, language, work style, and other differences are factors behind this people-focused disagreement. National norms, time issues, and inadequate communication all contribute to it.

    When project managers are assigned to such a project, they need to examine the norms and expectations from all different groups represented in the project. Training and experience will help them determine how deep the issues run and how easily they could be resolved. Improving communication is an excellent first step for many of these conflicts.

- **Task-focused**

    Finally, we have reached the type of disagreement that can be advantageous to the organization. When there are no disputes, the team may not realize that inefficiencies exist or know where they're located. Non-routine and complicated tasks especially benefit from differing opinions, so the team can scrutinize the issue more closely and take time to deliberate.

    However, even task-focused conflict—based on work and not on people—can still decrease the team's performance when the right ingredients are missing. For it to resolve in victory, there must be high trust among the team members. They should feel comfortable bringing up unpopular opinions. The team must be a safe and open space for all members to discuss their views. Thus, an attitude of collaboration is necessary.

PMs can encourage healthy conflict by allowing the team members to come to a resolution themselves, without interfering or micromanaging. They may also engage in "mining," or bringing sensitive topics to the forefront for the group to consider and discuss.

What happens when conflict isn't allowed to or just doesn't appear? One problem that often leads to a lack of necessary conflict is groupthink, which typically occurs when the team is homogenous and from similar backgrounds and experiences. Their decision-making is faulty because they don't consider alternatives, and they would rather be in harmony than make quality decisions that rest on disagreement.

NASA demonstrated this. Previous success in the space program led to complacency. The teams were cohesive and under pressure to make the right decisions, and they eventually fell into groupthink. Rather than criticizing each other's suggestions, finding alternatives, and asking for expert opinions, they censored themselves and rationalized their issues. Ultimately, groupthink was named as one of the root causes for the Columbia and Challenger failures (Villax, 2010).[12]

Resolving Conflicts

There are five strategies that a project leader and their team can use to work through conflict. Some are more likely to result in success, but unfortunately, not all methods will fit all situations. PMs need to decide which strategy would be best to use, depending on the scenario and circumstances. At some point, you will be the one held accountable for getting the team moving again, and you must take charge of that decision.

In order from most likely to encourage project success to least likely, here are the five techniques.

1. Win-win

This process is most desirable because all parties seek a win and understand that a win for others does not mean a loss for themselves. As a PM, unless you're involved directly in the situation, let the team work it out. It requires high trust levels among those working to find the solution, so everyone can be open and willing to discuss and collaborate.

"Win-win sees life as a cooperative arena, not a competitive one. Win-win is a frame of mind and heart that constantly seeks mutual benefit in all human interactions. Win-win means agreements or solutions are mutually beneficial and satisfying." —Stephen Covey[13]

When using this method, the team wants to find the best solution and not necessarily the one that would avoid hurting feelings or repressing valid viewpoints for the sake of team harmony. If the parties are not coming to a common solution, you should push their attention toward the positive aspects.

However, when you have two parties whose viewpoints are diametrically opposed, you may be unable to reach a win-win solution.

2. Compromise

The next most desirable technique is having all parties give up something to attain a mutually satisfying outcome. No one would get all that they want, but everyone can get at least something.

If the win-win technique doesn't work for one reason or another, the project manager can try to compromise. All parties must come to the table without too much power imbalance. They should be willing to make the necessary trade-offs because they want to find a solution.

3. PM decides

Sometimes as the project manager, you may need to force a solution. When parties cannot come to an agreement, it may be up to you to choose a solution. This can work when you're under deadline pressure and the people involved have drawn lines in the sand and aren't budging. They need to respect your decision and agree to abide by it for this to resolve the situation.

However, some people may feel resentment toward the outcome, and it could easily result in another conflict down the road. It's obviously not a preferred option, so you should only attempt this when neither of the first two methods has a chance of resulting in a favorable outcome.

4. Smoothing over/Facilitating

When the stakes are relatively low, but one side is entrenched in their position, you might consider using this method, which is merely another way of saying *pick your battles wisely*. Although emotions tend to run high in any conflict, some disagreements aren't worth spending much time and energy on. Finding the minimum common ground and moving forward is a decent way to deal with relatively unimportant battles.

As with forcing a decision, smoothing over the conflict won't necessarily resolve it permanently, and it often ends up reappearing in the future.

5. Withdrawal/Ignoring

The least favorable way to handle disagreement is to withdraw from it entirely. It's least effective because nothing gets resolved. You're kicking the can down the road, which usually results in its reappearance. The PM must be aware of whether one or more team members are dealing with apparent conflict before withdrawing from or ignoring it. That typically results in resentment and stress building up over time, and you want to head that off when possible.

In addition to having discussions with team members individually about what they're experiencing, you probably need to encourage more openness among the team. Promote issue raising and emotionally intelligent debate, which means that no one will be shamed for their views or be afraid to discuss them.

Key Takeaways

Although many people consider conflict to be a bad thing, when used healthily and constructively, it can increase the team's chance of success.

- Conflict is a feature, not a bug, so PMs need to deal with it constructively.

- Most people have a preferred way of handling conflict, but it may not be constructive, so they need to learn how to manage it for the team's benefit.

- Some types of conflict are inherently unhealthy—especially those that are focused on people—but a task-focused conflict should be encouraged and promoted in the right atmosphere.

- There are five methods for solving conflicts that project managers should be aware of, and two of them (win-win and compromise) are most likely to result in a constructive resolution of the issue.

In the next chapter, you will learn about building your ideal team.

---

[8] https://www.scientificamerican.com/article/why-our-brains-see-the-world-as-us-versus-them/
[9] https://www.pmi.org/learning/library/understanding-managing-conflict-resolution-strategies-6484
[10] https://www.planisware.com/hub/blog/conflict-management-guide-project-managers
[11] https://www.pmi.org/learning/library/understanding-managing-conflict-resolution-strategies-6484
[12] https://www.pmi.org/learning/library/understanding-managing-conflict-resolution-strategies-6484
[13] The 7 Habits of Highly Effective People by Stephen Covey, New York, NY 2013

CHAPTER 4

THERE IS NO "I" IN TEAM

AS a project leader, you need a reliable team that will collaborate with you to complete your project successfully. You may not always have the opportunity to select and hire your team members. However, you would still be instrumental in creating a team that works well together with the emotional space to address difficult issues and develop creative solutions to problems. The PM needs to manage the team in a way that promotes achievement and build it into a well-functioning unit.

The Importance of Teams

Groups of people working together have always been capable of achieving much larger goals than one person working alone. Hunters brought down large prey by working with each other, and one man didn't build the Great Pyramid of Giza.

In more recent years, as command-and-control leadership has fallen out of favor due to its limits on reacting quickly enough to changes on the ground, team members have taken on more responsibility to organize themselves and distribute the work. As a project manager, if you've ever worked in agile, you would know that this kind of self-organization is key to the success of those teams.

Today's businesses are sophisticated and have many relationships with other firms and organizations. The work is complex and highly detailed, and few people can master all intricacies involved in the project. Having a team of people who can tackle a problem and resolve it is necessary for getting work done and moving on to the next issue.

Globalization and technology put a lot of pressure on companies to adapt quickly and do everything better, faster, and cheaper. The modern world requires teams of people to collaborate to deal with these pressures.

Team Management

When the team is functioning like a well-oiled machine, it can be very productive. Successful project managers reduce tension within the team by addressing it when it occurs. They help everyone build trust with one another and remove any type of interpersonal grit that might otherwise get stuck in the gears and prevent the team from moving forward smoothly. It's critical to recognize that today's teams operate in an atmosphere of complexity and must spend more time with related issues and personnel because projects cannot operate in a vacuum.

In a study conducted on multiple projects within a three-year span, five factors were found to be fundamental for team success

(Thamhain, 2007).[14] Interestingly, they're not what managers often think of as being key to victory on a project, such as salary, the time the team has worked together, or project size and complexity. The critical factors are more about professional esteem and connecting goals to team members.

1. Most important: the work environment

To achieve the desired outcome, the project must provide professional challenges and stimulation to the team members. High performers aren't content to rest on their laurels or hit a career plateau. They also don't do well with routine tasks that don't provide any stimulation.

Doesn't it sound like the same requirements you have to be inspired as a project manager? Of course, there are often administrative and other bureaucratic tasks that you and the team must complete and that you'd prefer someone else to take care of. When you're running lean, however, you would still need to get them done.

These tasks are always mandatory, but make sure your team can spend enough time on interesting and demanding work.

2. Opportunities for recognition and accomplishments

Good team members want to achieve their goals, and recognition is often an essential part of that. The ability to list their accomplishments on a resume is a matter of pride.

Not to mention that it helps them further their careers. Just like you, competent team members aren't content to stagnate at one level or another. They want to explore and challenge themselves, and being able to point back to their achievements can help them find the next project or position that will allow them to progress further.

3. Ability to solve problems

If your team has difficulty making decisions or resolving issues, it's highly unlikely the members will be able to perform at the level you want. The team must not only have the capabilities of problem-solving, but they must also want to do it.

This requires a proactive approach. Occasionally, you could have a knowledgeable and competent team that can solve problems. However, rather than resolving the issues, the team might allow them to sit and fester unless they're explicitly told to address them. It is much better to have members interested in tackling issues—no matter the size—and clearing them up, so they can move on with their work.

4. Project related to organizational objectives

Positive results are easiest to achieve when the project itself aligns with the organization's core business and helps achieve its strategic objectives.

Securing visible management support is key to completing projects successfully, as you know. However, when the project doesn't affect management or can't see what's in it for them, there's no reason for them to support it. In fact, it's more of a nuisance to them than anything else. Senior executives also won't provide the resources you need because it won't align with their objectives and incentives.

Most people want to work on something that matters. What that means may be different for everyone, but the basic idea is that no one wants "make-work," which are tasks created to keep them busy with no real purpose.

Not having a meaningful project will make your life as a PM harder too. You may not have the resources you need, and you'll have a team that doesn't really want to work on the project. You'll feel like you're

trying to roll a boulder uphill every day. There's a difference between a challenge and an impossibility, and the impossible is not fun to work on.

5. Team members' skills and expertise match the project requirements

If you're working on an IT project, team members skilled in car manufacturing won't be a lot of help. You will mostly need coders and developers. Besides specialists in specific functional areas, you may need to include professionals experienced within the business, industry, or process.

Projects vary in complexity. Bringing in a team member who has worked only on simple projects in the past could be an issue when you have a complex one. No matter how smart they are, there's a learning curve they would need to go through first.

You may have a project that's complex, and no one has worked on anything similar before, even you. Rather than hiring team members with little experience, prefer those who participated in slightly less complex projects but have worked on more of them.

The study found other team factors contributing to a project win, such as team leadership, trust, and connection among the team members and clear project guidelines and expectations. You may have heard leaders talk about intrinsic and extrinsic motivators. The *intrinsic* ones are internal to each person and include a sense of working with purpose and being proud of accomplishments. *Extrinsic* are the motivators that managers can often provide, such as salary, bonuses, or time off. It's interesting that the most significant factors in successful teams are intrinsic rather than extrinsic.

It also provides some insight into how PMs can manage their teams best. Creating a supportive work environment is crucial to team success, and allowing team members to fulfill their professional dreams is a way for the project manager to support the team. Good communication is also essential, as it helps with stakeholders and builds mutual trust and respect among team members, which will help decrease unhealthy conflict.

As a PM, you will need to work with senior management to ensure the project is clearly aligned with business objectives, and that company-wide processes—such as purchasing and managerial controls—help the team rather than hinder it. You don't have much control over these policies and procedures, so you'll need to use influencing and persuading skills to get the most favorable environment possible for your team.

Team Improvement Techniques

Once you have a supportive work environment in place, there are other techniques that will help you manage the team. You must monitor each team member's performance, provide them with feedback, help resolve conflict as you learned in the last chapter, and determine whether there are changes you can make to improve the team's performance. You'll need a leader's emotional intelligence to provide feedback in a way that the team member can take it in and use it to improve rather than feel shamed for making a mistake.

- **Performance appraisals**

    The organization may have specific guidelines for writing your performance appraisals. This is a task that many project managers dread, but the procedure can be beneficial when applied appropriately. You help them see where they are having difficulty and make suggestions to help overcome it.

If you're happy with the performance, you will enjoy the appraisal process. You do need to let your good performers know that you are satisfied with what they're doing. You may still have a few suggestions for improvement and growth.

Many people find criticism hard to take, and you need to deliver it firmly, but not too harshly. One way to do this is to sandwich the critique. Give them a positive statement, then make your critique and follow up with another positive comment.

The appraisal won't be of much help if you don't mention specific situations and the work approach they can improve. You might set time aside for a brainstorming session to see if they have any ideas as well, then their goals can be determined appropriately.

- **Recognize and reward**

    I know old-school project managers used to say that rewards and recognition weren't necessary and that the satisfaction from a job well done was the only praise anyone would need.

    That's just not true. Even high performers need an occasional pat on the back or mention in a company-wide announcement for their accomplishments.

    This doesn't mean that everyone would get a trophy! However, those who truly do outstanding work or have achieved great things should be recognized for it.

    Remember that it's not just about the people receiving an award; it's about the people who watch them earn it. They may be inspired to reach higher in their own lives or see how high the bar is set for performance.

- **Observing and conversing**

    Step away from the computer. One of the most effective ways to manage people—particularly when they're high achievers—is to look at and speak with them. What are the issues they're having? What do they think is going well?

The more you can connect with your team members, the sooner you'll know if there's an issue. They'll be more willing to share their thoughts with you and the group and be more accountable when they know there's a space that is emotionally safe for them to do so.

Using BECC

Taking the above technique a little further, try BECC: Bond, Empathize, Connect, and Communicate (Wilson, 2020).[15] This technique will help you empower your team. As you bond and connect with them, you'll discover their strengths, which can be leveraged for the good of the team.

When you're clear on their capabilities, and you've communicated with them, so they understand what you want from them, you'll be more comfortable delegating specific tasks. Give them the power and authority to take on problems that they can resolve.

To be a true leader, you need to be thinking more about making your followers and team members successful and less about your own success. Their achievements (or lack thereof) will reflect back on you.

Tracking with an issue log

On a more mundane subject, you can manage the issues that arise on a project by creating a log to make sure nothing gets missed. You might end up assigning them to a team member or two to ensure they're resolved.

Team Building Stages

Successful projects begin with successful teams, and as a PM, you would lead the team-building effort. You may have team members who have worked together before, have a group of complete strangers, or mix the two. For them to collaborate and work well together, they need to know each other and their strengths and weaknesses. Your EQ as a project manager will give them some psychological space to come together as a team in an atmosphere of trust and respect.

In 1965, psychologist Bruce Tuckman developed the four-stage model for group development, adding on the fifth phase in 1977 (Toggl, n.d.)[16] They would run from the very beginning—when the team first meets—to the end of the project.

1. Forming

When you have a group of people who don't know each other, they can't even be considered a team at that point; it'd be more like a first date or orientation at a new job.

Everyone wants to make a good impression, meaning that they'll all be pleasant and polite to each other. They're excited about the new project and working with new people.

The project leader would use this time to set ground rules, talk about the overall vision, expected timeframe, and individual roles at a basic level. It's not usually a very productive time.

2. Storming

Now the reality of the project has hit everyone. What seemed challenging now may look nearly impossible to the team members, and the initial excitement has gone. It's also the time in many relationships when the quirks that you accepted when you didn't know the person have become incredibly annoying. Personality clashes often arise and team members may question other members or even the guidance of the project manager.

Here's where all your conflict management skills as a PM will come into play. Ensure that conflicts are resolved and not ignored to the best of your ability to avoid bigger issues later.

As you learned in the last chapter, disagreement is natural, and some of it is healthy. Allow the healthy ones to play out, empowering the team to handle them among themselves, and address the unhealthy ones that typically involve interpersonal relationships.

3. Norming

Once conflicts have been acknowledged and addressed, the team can settle down into a more cohesive unit. They may learn to appreciate each others' strengths, and they're starting to collaborate.

You might still see some issues with storming, as it's not always a smooth transition between the two stages, but the conflicts might be easier to deal with once there has been some cooperation.

4. Performing

If the team makes it this far, you will likely get a win on this project. Here they are collaborating, cooperating, and leveraging each other's strengths to be more productive.

They're confident and motivated to work toward the common goal. As a PM, you can feel comfortable delegating more work to them, knowing they're ready and willing to do it. They're eager to reach the destination and optimistic about their prospects.

This is the desired stage—one that many teams never achieve. Most accountability for team success or failure rests on you. If you're not clear on goals or roles and responsibilities in the forming stage,

the team will struggle to move through the storming phase. Similarly, if you don't handle the conflict well, the team may be unable to work as a cohesive unit in the norming stage of the process.

5. Adjourning/mourning

At the conclusion of the project, the team would disband. They may actually go through a mourning phase once they're finished with the project, or they may have enjoyed working with the other members and become sad about moving on to something else.

How to Build Your Performing Team

Now that you understand the phases of team development and skills you might need at each stage, you can think about how to develop a successful project team. What are the critical factors in building a team that would help you achieve the fourth stage of development: performing?

- **Choose the right people**

    If you have hiring authority, pick a solid group of people with diverse backgrounds. You will want teammates who challenge each other and avoid falling into groupthink. By the same token, you don't want a group full of divas trying to outshine the others at all costs, either.

    In addition—though, this may go without saying—you need to pick members whose skills and abilities match the project's requirements. You may find some applicants who have a lot of qualifications, at least on paper. But are they qualified for the position you need them to fill?

    Once you've hired them, take some time to discuss with them personally your expectations. Why do you think they're a good fit and their role on the team are some topics to discuss. This will help reduce the anxiety they're likely feeling about embarking on a new project.

- **Set the tone and ground rules**

    If you want the team members to raise difficult topics and feel comfortable owning their own mistakes, you need to demonstrate your high EQ in the beginning. While the team is forming, make sure they understand what you expect from them and what the rules are.

    If there are ambiguities around roles and responsibilities, address them. Now's the time to make goals and roles crystal clear, so no one would be confused or feeling like someone isn't pulling their weight. Bringing clarity while they're forming will help defuse some tension while storming.

- **Communicate a clear vision**

    Likewise, everyone should know exactly what the overall goal is and what they are expected to achieve. You want every person on the team to achieve a win. All individual goals should add up to the overall project goal.

    Remember—you're the ship's captain. The crew members need to know where they're rowing, so they all can head in the same direction. You're the one with the bird's-eye view.

- **Pick small wins**

    If there's an opportunity to celebrate achievements early on, do it. This would be another way to defuse some conflicts in the storming stage. It keeps people motivated when the project hits what appears impossible after the forming phase has ended.

Plan for these small goals early on and make them ones that you believe can be achieved. Reaching them encourages the team going forward and gives them a sense of pride in their work.

- **Be transparent**

    You already know how important communication is to project success. Your team members should be the first to hear any news, after you. Keep them up to date on what's happening with the larger client organization (where it's relevant) and issues that you hear about from the stakeholders.

    The spirit of collaboration that you've fostered should provide an open space for team members to share rather than hoard information. The more clarity you can have with them, the less pressured they are to hold back or release information selectively.

- **Provide feedback after meetings**

    We discussed performance appraisals in a previous section, but more targeted feedback can assist the team as well. There's a place for one-on-ones, but make sure you make space for group feedback as well. Remember the compliment sandwich when you have critiques, so the team won't feel ashamed for making errors.

- **Provide scheduled team-building time**

    You'll be working with the team a lot during the forming phase, both as a whole and with individual team members one-on-one. Even after they've settled into the norming stage, continue to set aside time for team building.

    Small business owners are usually encouraged to set aside time to work *on* their business, not just *in* it. In other words, it is not only about fulfilling customer orders or providing the service, but also about planning and reviewing. Similarly, all should work *on* the team and not just *in* the project.

As noted earlier, you don't have to go off-site, though the occasional evening out or fun activity isn't a bad idea, particularly when morale is flagging. Some of this time could be devoted to short meetings where the team would reflect on what's gone well and what hasn't, then brainstorm ideas for improvement.

How to Break Barriers

There are common barriers that get in the way of effective team building. Fortunately, that means there are also different ways of reducing or even eliminating them as well.

1. Varying viewpoints and judgments of team members

You followed the guidelines on hiring a diverse team, and now interpersonal relationships are threatening the team's success.

- Try to uncover these issues early in the forming stage to address them quickly.
- Give them a very clear station WII-FM (What's In It For Them), so they understand how they will benefit personally from the project.
- Explain how their roles, responsibilities, and interests meld with the overall goal.

2. Ambiguity in roles

This may be less of an issue in waterfall project management, where you would usually be the one responsible for assigning who does what. However, with self-organizing teams, this is sometimes more difficult.

- When you sit down with them individually, understand where they believe themselves to fit within the group.
- Create a work breakdown structure (WBS), so the tasks and associated responsibilities are clear, then assign people as necessary.
- Monitor potential role conflicts throughout the project.

3. Lack of clarity on goals

This burden is on you to a large extent. If you didn't get clarity with the client on what they wanted, you should have continued asking questions until you got it. If you're clear on what they are, but your team members aren't, what you have here is a failure to communicate.

- Keep asking your client/sponsor for more details and reasons.
- Inform your team members and let them ask questions.

4. Changing environments

To some extent, circumstances change over which you have no control. However, there may be other dynamics—such as a desire by the client to squeeze out a little more from the deliverable—that you can resolve as an effective PM.

- Ensure critical stakeholders clarify the overall direction and get the team's buy-in.
- Communicate the dangers of unwarranted changes to the client and their senior management, which will help stabilize the environment.
- Develop your contingency plans.

5. Leadership competition

Similar to role ambiguity, this may be less apparent in traditional project management. Otherwise, in this case, you may not be performing up to the expectations of your team.

- Senior management needs to demonstrate their support of the team lead.
- As a PM, understand what the team expects from you and adjust accordingly. Having clear roles, as noted above, will also help.

6. Lack of structure and definition on the team

Not only does senior management need to be educated and "sold" on the project team, but so does the team itself.

- Senior management and the client must demonstrate their visible support in emails, newsletters, videos, among other forms of social communication.
- Hold regular team meetings.

7. Lack of commitment by team members

As soon as this issue arises, it needs to be addressed. There are a variety of reasons why a member of the team may hold negative views on the project or team itself. The issue is often insecurity, but it could also be a relationship conflict or because the project doesn't satisfy them professionally.

- If they're insecure, try to figure out why and help them allay their fears.
- With a relationship conflict, handle it as you learned in the last chapter as soon as you can.
- If they may be better off elsewhere on a different project that aligns more with their interests, consider finding a replacement.

8. Choosing the wrong people

Depending on who has hiring authority, this may or may not be due to your staffing decisions.

- Negotiate assignments to try to leverage each member's strengths.
- Clarify WII-FM, including the potential rewards, purpose of the project, and rules of engagement.
- If it still doesn't work out, consider replacing them.

9. Project leader credibility

To want to follow you, team members must respect your authority and abilities. If they don't see you as credible, you'll need to repair that image of yourself if you want to move to the performing stage.

- Get visible support from senior management.
- Demonstrate your decision-making and problem-solving skills to the team.
- Demonstrate your technical knowledge.

10. Communication issues

You know how important it is. If you're having difficulty or don't think the team is where it needs to be regarding this skill, try the following.

- Hold regular status reviews and use schedules and the reporting system to facilitate transparency.
- Where you can, colocate the team: have everyone in the same room together.
- Establish regular channels and schedules for conversations with clients and senior management. Ensure key agreements and issues are noted in writing.

11. Lack of support from senior executives

If you read the first book of this bundle, you learned some techniques for ensuring that you have senior management on board visibly with the team and project.

- Invite them to be a part of the project reviews.

- Ensure they understand what you and the team need from them.

- Develop relationships with key members and sell them on the project's importance for them personally; yes, senior management needs to know WII-FM too!

When you have a high-performing team, it truly captures the spirit of the old adage that *"The whole is greater than the sum of its parts."* Teams that collaborate together achieve significant synergies. Make it so helping each other and cooperating are natural for the team and not considered extra work or a burden. They understand that when they function as a unit and not separate people coming together, they can achieve more, both in terms of the project and for their individual development.

Key Takeaways

The team's function is critical to project success, and project managers should encourage members by managing and building the team according to successful principles.

- Effective team management involves PMs with high emotional intelligence to create an environment of openness and trust.

- There are five stages of team development, and many teams, unfortunately, don't reach the crucial fourth phase known as "performing," where they would act effectively and as a well-oiled machine.

- During team development, the project manager must continuously build the team and work through common barriers to performance.

In the next chapter, you will learn how to develop each member, so they can be their best selves on the project and work to their strengths.

---

[14] https://www.pmi.org/learning/library/managing-project-teams-age-complexity-7212
[15] https://www.ntaskmanager.com/blog/effective-team-management/
[16] https://toggl.com/stages-of-team-development/

CHAPTER 5

PUT ME IN, COACH, I'M READY TO PLAY

AS the *leader* of your project team—not just the manager—you are responsible for developing your team members. You know by now that the top-down management style of the last century is no longer in fashion, and even waterfall PMs are directing their teams less and empowering them more.

On an effective team, members handle most daily tasks and responsibilities, solve work problems, and resolve interpersonal conflicts themselves. This frees up the project manager to handle big-picture tasks and deal with higher-level issues. The more you can trust your team to handle tactical work, the more you can focus on the strategic.

However, your team may not be ready to handle these tasks right away or believe they're prepared. Assuming that you have hired mature team members with a strong work ethic, your focus should be on mentoring and encouraging them rather than directing and micromanaging.

What is Coaching?

As mentioned earlier, one measure of success of your leadership is how much the team flourishes under your guidance. The better they do, the more their results will reflect on you and vice versa; if the team performs poorly, most will assume your weak leadership is a primary contributing factor.

Coaching is correcting behaviors to increase the chances of reaching a goal successfully, whether that be personal or business-related. It's positive and constructive in nature. Top athletes use coaches to improve some aspect of their performance in the sport, and they may have more than one coach to work on different skills. Business executives also use coaches to help them be mature in various areas and level up their performance. It's not the same as mentoring, which we'll discuss a little later in the chapter.

In addition to typical project management skills, such as planning and organizing, a good PM must also be a good coach. Though they may jump in whenever they see the team falling behind or not using resources effectively, there are a handful of areas where PMs typically have the opportunity to help team members improve (Woods et al., 2011).[17]

- Strategic thinking
- Interpersonal skills
- Managing conflict
- Leadership
- Communication
- Versatility

What Benefits Can Team Members See from PM Coaching?

When the project manager coaches, in conjunction with team building, the team can achieve powerful results. Team members are more likely to accept additional tasks. Team building allows for coaching to take place in a constructive and positive environment, which would then lead to working *smarter*, not *harder*.

When one team member is underperforming, coaching can help them learn how to contribute more to the team. Those who are already solid performers learn to share their knowledge with the rest of their teammates and help teach them how to be more productive. Just as a Six Sigma Master Black Belt coaches other Black Belts, the PM can help star performers learn to coach their peers. Leveraging all team resources and sharing knowledge so no information is lost if a star performer leaves is a contingency plan that all project managers should make.

Another valuable bonus of coaching is that it empowers the team. Members learn to think independently and solve problems on their own, which would increase the trust and pride they have in their work, in addition to taking some of the burden from the project manager.

When you develop the project plan, you will be identifying the competencies needed for the various tasks in the project. When you're choosing your team members, ensure they are *coachable*. In other words, they need to be willing to be coached. Some people aren't, maybe because they believe they know everything or for some other reason. Avoid hiring those types of people if you can.

It's not a "one-and-done" effort. With one short talk, it's unlikely you'll be able to turn an underperforming member into a star. Recognize that you'll need to spend regular time with them to get the results you want. Just as team building needs to occur throughout the entire project, so do coaching activities.

Also, assess the willingness of your team members. You may need to build more trust with them before they can be vulnerable to working with you. Evaluate whether coaching is really what the person needs. If they're having difficulty managing their conflicts with other team members, that's one thing; however, if they also can't do their work on time and have poor communication and interpersonal skills, they may need more help than you can give them. Consider having a talk with their supervisor or HR, or replacing them.

Coaching Principles

You can work with your people either one-on-one or as a team. It can be formal or informal as well. If it's formal, you'll probably have a structured way to approach it and a feedback process too. You'll generate reports and set goals to be accomplished. The informal process is more of a catch-as-catch-can model, where you would discuss goals and challenges the person or team is currently facing.

You would set the tone for constructive and positive feedback while supporting the team consistently. As they build trust with you, the coaching effort will become much more relaxed. There are many different frameworks out there, complete with catchy acronyms. Your organization may have one that it wants you to follow, or you could read about it. Whichever one you choose, there are some common characteristics for being an effective coach.

- **Active listening**

    It's not about you and your knowledge, which is the foundation of mentoring instead. In the coaching process, the team member should be talking more while you guide them.

- **Socratic method**

    This form of teaching relies on asking questions. You don't want to give your team members the answers; you want them to figure it out for themselves. Their answers may differ from what you might initially think. They also need to be right for them—not for you.

    Help them reach the answers by asking questions designed to get them thinking.

- **Stimulating inspiration**

    Help your team members be creative and inspired. Keep the focus on them and not you.

- **Flexible**

    Because this process is designed to develop team members, the answers and questions may not be the same for everyone. Even if you're using an existing coaching model, make sure you tailor everything to the person or team you're working with at that moment.

- **Humble**

    You may be surprised by the creative and workable solutions your people can come up with during the process! Understanding that you don't know everything is crucial—not just for building trust, but also allowing them to be emotionally open as well.

- **Focus on the process**

    It's natural for action-oriented personalities to want to have the result completed yesterday. However, that won't be the reality, especially when you're coaching. It takes time for new good habits to form, and your underperformer won't transform into a rock star overnight.

Therefore, look at small improvements. Did your conflict-averse team member stand up for themselves in a meeting? That's progress. Did the person who lacks interpersonal skills make a small step toward recognizing another team member for their hard work? Progress. Track the little improvements, and you'll see that they add up over time.

- **Mutually defined outcomes**

    Managers may tell their staff about the outcomes they expect, but coaches don't. Instead, they work with the participant or team to define the ideal result. Both of you need to trust each other for this to work. They must believe that you have their best interests at heart and are committed to the outcome that you'll both be defining.

Types of Coaching

There are several different types of coaching that are often used within the project management process.

1. Knowledge building

This is the easiest type of coaching and results in the team member obtaining the knowledge they need for the specific project or task—for example, training on project management software. It's used best for new staff or when a new technique or tool is introduced.

2. Soft skills acquisition

Many people have gaps in these skills, which include communication, leadership, and relationship building. This can be done either formally or informally, and individually or with the whole team.

Focusing on soft skills works well when there is conflict within the team or individual members are disengaged from the project or culture.

3. Work-life balance

Why should you, as a PM, provide this kind of coaching? You want to avoid burnout in your team members, for one thing. Don't worry—you won't be a therapist or counselor, but you'll discuss activities such as stress management and self-confidence.

It requires a higher level of and mutual trust between you and the team member than knowledge or skill building. Use it when you have a team member who is dealing with a life issue or seems so stressed out that their work is being affected.

4. Performance

Here's where you would assist your team members with achieving a project goal or objective. It differs from knowledge building because you would have a particular result that you want to achieve rather than general knowledge. An example of performance coaching is working with a team member in conducting successful stakeholder analysis interviews.

5. Stretch/developmental

This is the toughest and most time-consuming way to coach someone, and it requires dedication from both parties. It helps them develop personally, so they can take on more rewarding and challenging projects.

Once you've selected which type of coaching will be most appropriate, you can move through the phases of coaching with them. Bear in mind that since this kind of work often requires multiple sessions to obtain results, you could end up going through the same phases more than once or from one stage back to a previous one to ensure that your coaching sticks.

Coaching Procedures

Some of your team members may need direction. For them, you may need to provide answers or specific instructions for certain tasks. Others may respond better to supportive coaching, where you would spend more time on facilitating new behaviors or building self-confidence. Whether you direct or support in your coaching, you will depend on the person you're coaching and what they need to address.

1. Observe

As a project manager, you should be taking the opportunity to watch your entire team in action. Specifically, you may find someone who isn't keeping up or not displaying the same skills as their peers.

2. Identify gaps

What type of coaching does the person need? They may lack the knowledge, skills, or even self-confidence to perform well. As you determine what they need, you can then identify the kind of coaching they need.

3. Validate

Verify what you've observed with managers and supervisors. You may or may not need to ask some open-ended questions, because their manager could demonstrate that they are also concerned about the team member's gap.

4. Engage

After you've confirmed the person does require particular coaching, invite them to join you. Remember that, although they may have a need, they may not be willing yet to engage in a coaching relationship with you. Clarify for them what your expectations are for the process and how it will work.

5. Collaborate

Once they're OK with engaging with you, share your observations and what you believe the gap is. Notice that this stage is called *collaboration*, not direction! Help them arrive at the conclusion they want to address and improve their performance. Together, decide what help will be required and what the actions should be.

6. Agree

Both of you need to concur on the action plan, goals, and outcomes. Your team member must be willing to put in the work, which means that they understand the plan to be fair and reasonable and take personal responsibility for self-development. You need to see that the plan will serve to make the necessary improvements.

7. Give feedback

Be specific in your constructive criticisms or praise, as appropriate. They need to understand exactly what it is that they're doing wrong or right, so they can either fix it or make sure they incorporate it into their work habits.

They need to know they're on the right track, so make sure you *praise* when you see progress. Most people respond much better to praise than criticism, so make sure you take the opportunity when it arises.

8. Monitor

Just as it's easy for the company to lapse on the progress it's made from making changes, so too can people. Follow up periodically to ensure they haven't slipped back into their old ways and have maintained their progress.

Mentoring Your Team Members

Mentoring is an essential skill that leaders need. A mentor is a trusted advisor to their mentee and guides them either formally or informally toward professional growth and development. In contrast to a coaching relationship, mentoring is about you as a project manager and the specific skills and knowledge you would share with the person you mentor. It requires a longer time commitment and can last from several months to even years.

Not everyone on your team will necessarily want to be in a mentoring relationship, and some of them may not wish to be in one with you. Don't take it personally—understand those team members may want another perspective. You don't want to force anyone into it because they won't want to do the work.

Some organizations set up formal programs for mentorship. Programs support the business objectives and strategic plan for the firm. They may have criteria for mentors in terms of training, ensuring that time is set aside regularly for both parties to meet, providing an orientation for all employees, and overall support from various levels of management.

Smaller companies—or those that have not yet matured in terms of projects—often don't have formal programs set up, so mentorship would occur informally. It's up to the two involved to figure out how to schedule the time to get together, and it's pretty common for the mentee to initiate these types of relationships.

In that case, the mentee should communicate why they want a mentor (e.g., to help with technical skills or navigate a large company's bureaucracy). They would define the background and skills the mentor should pose, identify possible candidates and contact them to see if they might work with them, and follow up with the person who looks promising.

Note that although mentorship is expected from leaders, including project managers, you can also still be someone else's mentee even as you're serving as a mentor. You have the knowledge and skills to guide someone relatively new to project management, but you may want to level up your own skills by working with a program manager who has more extensive experience.

There are several different ways that a mentor can advise their protege, and these can also be combined, depending on the relationship.

- **Source of information**

    The mentor might suggest good professional organizations to join or books to read and helpful conferences that their mentee can attend.

- **Career guide**

    As a PM, you can recommend credentials that someone in the field should have, the types of projects to take on that can satisfy their career goals, and courses they should take. If you're helping someone who wants to follow in your footsteps, you can provide a wealth of information in that regard.

- **Interpersonal guide**

    Effective project managers understand that politics comes along with the job. Someone may need your help navigating informal networks in your organization, or you might assist them in understanding political influencers and how to leverage them.

- **Intellectual guide**

    Here, you'll be helping someone with some of the more technical skills of project management. They might come to you for advice on a specific task or give them feedback on their work. You can then collaborate with them, perhaps on something like a paper for a project management conference. This type of mentoring can be the most helpful in the project management field (Levin, 2011).[18]

Grow as a Mentor

Being trained as a mentor can be helpful when you want to give back to the profession in that way or if your organization requires it. If you need to obtain the training on your own, look for a program that contains the following elements:

- How to develop and document goals with the mentee.
- How to set short-term and long-term goals, with the short-term ones designed specifically for early wins.
- How to develop appropriate metrics to measure success.
- Using open-ended questions to guide the discussions and keep them on track.
- Further developing the mentor's relationship skills, including critical thinking and active listening.
- Using feedback approaches known to foster trust and confidence.
- Working with different generations and personalities.
- Understanding the mentor's personal style.

According to Levin, there are **five characteristics** that a good mentor needs to develop, so their mentees can be successful.

1. A genuine interest in the mentee

This might be more difficult in organizations where mentoring relationships are assigned. However, if the mentor can't develop an actual interest in their mentee's growth and success, it will be hard for them to find the time necessary to meet and mentor them.

2. Being a role model

In other words, the mentor needs to practice what they preach. They should demonstrate behavior and attitude that the organization determines as keys to success. Good mentors lead by example, in addition to providing feedback and advice.

Anyone whose motto is "Do as I say, not as I do" would be a very poor mentor.

3. Providing assistance

As part of the process, be prepared to offer resources, suggestions, and assistance with problem solving. You could discuss examples or stories of previous projects, how similar issues were handled, and the results from the approach taken. People respond very well to stories, so use them when you can.

4. Giving constructive criticism

If you are afraid to be truthful with someone because it might hurt their feelings, you should probably not offer yourself up as a mentor when asked. You need to be clear about what went wrong or what needs improvement; otherwise, the mentee will be unable to grow.

On the other hand, you don't want to crush their spirit either, so you'll need to communicate your feedback supportively. Show them how they can learn from the problem and improve rather than be upset or hindered by a mistake.

Just as with coaching, praise when you have the chance. Make it specific, so they can understand what can put them on the right track.

5. Assisting with motivation

Encourage your mentee to do what's necessary to grow professionally. You might suggest steps they can take to improve their conflict resolution if you see that to be an issue, which will help them solve problems better. Achieving long-term goals takes time, so help them with the small steps they would need to take along the way.

People and Cultures

You may or may not be used to working with project members from a variety of countries or cultures. As companies have globalized, they often need to have project teams made up of staff from different offices around the world. PMs must be comfortable acknowledging and working with these differences, so the team can work cohesively in the performing stage.

Cultures differ in many ways, not just language; you have to be aware of how others think, conduct nonverbal communication, their values, and their behaviors. For example, it's pretty well known that Eastern cultures tend to prioritize the group over the individual, and in the West, it's usually the other way around. In some cultures, women may look down when the PM speaks to them, which is an indication of respect and not shyness. Otherwise, they may not verbally disagree with you when you're talking, which does not actually mean that they agree with you or understand what you've said.

There are differences between generations as well. Generation X (born roughly between 1961 and 1980) and younger generations are more accustomed to a multicultural workplace and having women in positions of authority. Baby Boomers (born 1946-1960) and older do not necessarily have the same level of understanding.

Typical problems that project managers have with multicultural teams include a lack of understanding of all the present cultures, inability to open communication channels between all team members, and ignoring team members' needs whose cultures they're not familiar with. Also, there are often miscommunications and misconceptions among the team members themselves, which lead to conflict and delay.

As a project manager, you can ask yourself how you can interact with each member of the team effectively. How can you open up communication and help resolve some of the inevitable cultural conflicts?

- **Understand the cultures present in your team**

    The best way for a project manager to handle the diversity on their teams is to educate themselves. Recall that a diverse team brings more creative solutions, as long as the environment is psychologically safe for everyone to speak up.

- **Attend cross-cultural workshops and training**

    Given that so many companies have global locations, more resources are dedicated to teaching people how to thrive and help others thrive in these relationships.

- **Be humble**

    Just because you're used to doing things in a certain way doesn't mean that another culture's method is inferior. Demonstrate your openness to learning new things and encourage the team to do the same.

- **Raise difficult issues when necessary**

    Just as you shouldn't ignore conflict that needs to be aired out, don't ignore the elephant in the room. Maybe the entire team needs to attend cross-cultural training, or you have to be the one to raise the issue, so others can feel comfortable discussing it. Don't sweep these kinds of problems under the rug because they will come back to bite you.

Delegation

When you have a team whose members you trust to do their best and solve problems creatively, you'll discover how easy and freeing delegation can be. It's a well-known productivity hack in other fields, and to be a successful project leader, you must master the art of delegating to others.

It's not something that comes naturally for many people. Especially for high performers, because they're used to doing things themselves when trying to make sure the task reaches its best standards. If you are a great expert in some field and want to do it all by yourself, then you should be a team member rather than a project manager.

It's important to note that even though you may delegate a task to someone else, you're still ultimately responsible for it. If the person you delegate to doesn't get it done or performs poorly, that will reflect badly on you. This is another reason why people tend not to delegate: they don't want someone else doing anything wrong when they could simply do the task themselves in the first place.

Why delegate then? What are the benefits that would outweigh the concerns?

- **You don't have time for everything**

    As you know, numerous tasks, duties, and obligations come with the role of a PM. We've discussed the importance of the project manager remaining strategic and taking charge of the high-level vision and execution of the project. When you focus on that, you'll have less time for more tactical or daily tasks.

    You know that your team doesn't have the same overall view of the project that you do, but instead, it has knowledge and skills for daily tasks. Which would make more sense to you—keeping

your focus on the strategic vision or performing tasks that your team members are qualified to do?

- **You don't know everything**

    True leaders are humble and know what they don't know. They understand that they and others will make mistakes, and their ideas aren't always the best ones. That's why they include the team when they're brainstorming solutions for problems.

    Once you accept that others also have good ideas, how would you know that the way you approach a particular task is best? Maybe the person you're considering delegating a specific task to is an expert in that field, productive, or has otherwise uncovered the secrets to getting the job done quickly. Maybe they don't, but you won't really know until you give them the task, which would also free up your time to work on something else.

- **As a leader, you're responsible for the growth of your direct reports**

    No one needs robots on a project management team. The PM and all members need to have good critical thinking and problem-solving capabilities while always working on improvement.

    Delegating tasks to your team members gives them a new challenge they can be proud of once they've completed it and potentially a new tool to add to their toolbox. By letting go of something that you know you can do, you provide someone else the opportunity to stretch themselves.

    This is all really what leading a team is all about. It's not about having people who would come in and do the same job day in and day out, but instead, it's about helping them grow. If you don't delegate, you deny your team a chance to develop professionally.

Delegate Tasks with Three Steps

There are three process steps to delegating a task (Stickney et al., 1983).[19]

1. Assign responsibility

First, you must choose who will take on the task, preferably someone you trust and with whom you have a reasonable expectation that they'll complete the job on time. Make sure it will provide them a growth opportunity too.

Try to distribute the rote tasks and more exciting ones equally among the team.

2. Provide the authority

Give the team member the right to act on your behalf and with whatever permissions or resources they need to do so. If anyone should know that the team member owns a particular task, let them know ahead of time.

Also, ensure they have the necessary budget. Avoid sending a team member out to the office supply store to buy whiteboard markers without giving them money for those supplies.

3. Create accountability

There must be a way for you and any other relevant stakeholders to know when the task has been accomplished.

How Best to Delegate

Right now, you may understand the importance of delegation but still be unsure as to how to go about it. Here are some ways to improve your delegating prowess and become more confident in offloading these tasks.

- **Pick the right tasks**

    There may be some tasks that are more difficult to delegate, or for whatever reason, you truly need to keep them for yourself. Tasks that you can assign easily tend to be finite and discrete with clear timeframes and endpoints.

    Ideally, they would also be tactical rather than strategic in nature, and the team member chosen has some familiarity with the topic, even if they haven't performed it before.

- **Share clarity**

    Not having clear guidelines is a recipe for failure in management. If you can't describe it accurately, don't assign it until you can be precise.

    Explain any key or starting points and make sure the team member understands all relevant deadlines—not just the one specific to the task but also any others that could impact it. Both of you should know when the job is done.

- **Don't micromanage the "how"**

    Once your team member understands the task, let them run with it. What's important is the quality of the end result—not how they got there.

    You can provide templates if you think they'll be helpful, but that doesn't mean the team member must use them if they can complete it on their own.

- **Be available for assistance without being a "helicopter parent"**

    In other words, don't hover. The point of delegation is to free up your time for the more strategic obligations that you may have, and watching them working isn't one of those duties.

On the other hand, your team member may need assistance or have questions for you. You can also check in by asking for a draft if they're working on a document or speech. Don't let them believe they've been left on their own to do your work.

- **Team be praised!**

  Be generous and public with your praise, and make sure you're rewarding both effort and outcomes. Share in meetings and emails that the whole team reads. Hopefully, with all the delegation distributed evenly among team members, there will be frequent opportunities to mention everyone's good work throughout the project.

- **No "backsies"**

  If you've chosen tasks that will stretch your team members, they may struggle with it. If someone tries to give it back to you, try to figure out why they're having a problem. Are they feeling overwhelmed by all their responsibilities or by the challenge you provided? Are they disengaging from the project or just being uncooperative? Avoid taking it back unless doing so will prevent a major disaster.

  If delegation is a challenge for you—as it is for so many people—don't allow yourself to take back that task, even if it means a little more work on your part to help your team member get through it. You'll get better at delegating, and they'll grow too with the challenge you've provided. Stay strong.

Key Takeaways

One of the critical components behind being a good leader is developing the individual team members working on the project *with you*.

- Coaching is a relationship where you would help team members improve project-related skills, which may include conflict management and handling interpersonal relationships.

- Mentoring is how you would help guide an individual toward the right opportunities for their career and personal development.

- Multicultural teams often run into issues due to their diversity, and there are ways the PM can help the team work together, despite their differences.

- Good leaders must delegate to their team members, both to free up time better spent on strategic initiatives for themselves and help the team grow.

In the next chapter, you will learn how to get the best from your resources.

---

[17] https://www.pmi.org/learning/library/project-manager-team-coach-plan-success-6251
[18] https://www.pmi.org/learning/library/mentoring-key-competency-program-project-professionals-6264
[19] https://www.pmi.org/learning/library/delegation-sharing-authority-matrix-organizations-1806

CHAPTER 6

LEVEL UP YOUR BEST

THERE are two essential skills that project managers must have to leverage their resources as best they can: *negotiation* and *facilitation*. As with many of the leadership techniques discussed in this book, these are useful tools to have in your personal life as well.

Want to buy a car? Know how to get a better price. Want a higher salary? Know how to start the conversation and demonstrate your value. Want to tackle a specific project? Know what they want from the project and what you can offer as a tradeoff. Want to have a better relationship with your teenage child? Learn to navigate what they can and can't handle, so they can participate in important decisions.

Negotiation

It's a complex skill, but you won't get far without it. It combines many other leadership characteristics, including emotional and traditional intelligence, strategic and tactical thinking, focus on results, ability to listen actively, and conflict management. You can negotiate the scope with stakeholders, prices with vendors, responsibilities with team members, budget with the controllers, and get the best employees from their managers. You may be called upon to negotiate changes in scope during the project, the release to operations, roles and responsibilities, and the boundaries of authority, among other issues.

Put simply, negotiation is how you would find a mutually agreeable solution for a problem that's shared between people.

At this point I would like to encourage you to download the negotiation checklist, which I created as a bonus to this book. You can find a banner with a link at the beginning of this book. The following sections are summarized on the checklist. It will be practical for you when you need to enter negotiation, whether it is on the project or any area of life and need to remember the most important tips and techniques.

There are generally three styles of negotiating (Englund, 2010).[20]

1. Hard

This is a typical negotiating style for those who believe that resources are limited and only one side can get them, which means if you win, then I lose. It's an aggressive approach where the other side would be the enemy.

The hard negotiator bargains competitively to make sure they win; otherwise, they lose. There is no in-between, nor is there a way for all parties involved to come out on top.

2. Soft

Naturally, the opposite of hard is soft. These negotiators—who often tend to be conflict-avoidant—give up more than they should. They believe that the relationship with the other party is more important than what they might get out of the deal.

Pleasing the other side becomes the goal, which results in an agreement reached easily. However, the soft bargainer loses much more than they gained, and the deal they made becomes more than likely a bad one.

Note that there is still no concept of a win-win here in terms of deal outcomes.

3. Principled

By contrast, the principled one sets aside the personalities and relationships from the problem at hand. Rather than focusing on positions, they look toward interests instead.

What's the difference between interests and positions? If I'm going car shopping, I might take up a *position* that I would only purchase a four-door sedan. However, what I actually want from my new car is a place to put my bicycle, so I can drive to the park and go biking. That's my *interest*.

A smart car salesperson will winkle out of me what I really want out of the car—what my true *interest* is—and start making recommendations aimed at my real desire. I might drive out of the showroom in a two-door, zippy coupe with a trunk rack that is more expensive than the original four-door I was looking at. Still, the salesperson has satisfied my desire and their interest in a higher commission.

Principled negotiators generate several options that could potentially satisfy both parties, rather than argue about one option that would clearly favor one side over the other. They make the agreement based on objective reasons and not a desire to please another or crush the competition.

They understand the other party's **Best Alternative To a Negotiated Agreement (BATNA)**. In other words, if you can't reach an agreement, what is the best thing they can do instead? Similarly, you would also know your best alternative if you had to walk away, and you improve it if you can.

Life is not pie; more for one person does not have to mean less for another. In many negotiations, people tend to assume that they would either win or lose, which are the only two options. However, there's often another.

The third alternative is a win-win, where the solution would benefit both parties. It may be harder to find and require more discussion and potentially more time brainstorming the issue. If a win-win cannot be found, the next best thing would be a compromise, where the loss is made as small as possible and distributed evenly.

Stages of Negotiation

Typically, there are five stages to the agreement.

1. Decide to negotiate

First, identify the problem, with negotiation as its solution. You may not want to negotiate every issue; remember the importance of picking your battles.

2. Prepare

There are things you'll need to know before sitting down at the table with your fellow negotiators. Understand the problem itself and your goals for the solution. Are you trying to solve for low costs? What is the ideal outcome for your team?

If you have others supporting you during the process, ensure everyone's roles and responsibilities are clear.

It's crucial to know your own BATNA. If the other side won't give in, or for whatever reason you need to walk away, know what you'll do instead. In the car example, if that salesperson cannot give you what you want, you'll just have to go to a different dealership.

Strengthen yours if you can, then you know you won't agree to anything out of desperation because your BATNA is still a good alternative. It gives you more leverage.

By the same token, understand what the other side's BATNA is and find arguments to make it appear worse if you can. If they need to make the agreement with you, because their alternative is much worse, you've given yourself more leverage.

3. Negotiate

For a successful negotiation, find a third alternative that's ideally a win-win for all parties involved. You'll probably need to brainstorm additional options for everyone to choose from or modify into a win-win.

This stage often requires time and patience. If you cannot get what you want right away, that doesn't mean you should bring a halt to the negotiations. If your BATNA leaves you free to walk away, use that leverage to keep the others at the table.

Once everyone has accepted a specific option, make sure it is captured in writing. Verify that everyone has agreed—especially if someone has remained silent. They may have reservations about it that could cause them to ignore any eventual action plan.

Develop a plan outlining what each party will do with the timeframe and make sure it's clear who would do what. Build in compliance with the written plan, so everyone knows how they'll demonstrate that they kept to the agreement.

4. Implement

Make sure you congratulate everyone for a successful negotiation without gloating; you don't want to burn your bridges. In today's world, people's paths can cross multiple times. Don't make enemies when you don't need to.

Then, the plan needs to be carried out as agreed by all parties.

5. Follow-up

Nurture the relationships you've made. If you could reach a win-win, the parties should then be willing to fulfill promises.

Monitor to make sure all parties are abiding by the agreement.

Guidelines for Successful Negotiations

Although each negotiation is different, there are common elements to those that successfully achieve the parties' goals and result in a win-win. Learning how to interact with others without either acquiescing or becoming too assertive is something that you can practice in everyday life, not to mention the projects you're leading.

- **Three Ps: be prepared, positive, and patient**

    Avoid being caught by surprise, knowing how processes could go wrong or take too long. Prepare; have contingency and risk management plans in place. Ensure that you gather information from everyone involved to understand fully how alternative agreements might impact the work.

    People find it easy to deal with the people they like, so when you bring a positive attitude, your negotiation partners will be more positive in their interactions with you too.

When it comes to negotiations, you need to be patient. Sometimes, you may feel like shutting it down or moving on to something that isn't so uncomfortable. Resist these urges. Take time to answer questions about how a proposed new process would work or allow the other party to think through the implications of the option you offered them.

Likewise, make sure you take time to comprehend their offer and its consequences, along with any second and third-order consequences that could arise.

- **Know your opening offer and your bottom line**

    This aligns with being prepared. Give yourself some room to negotiate rather than starting with your bottom line.

    For example, if you think the project will take between four to six months, don't open with four months or fewer. The other side could ask for three months, and you won't have room to adjust.

    When you have limits, you'll know when it's time to walk away. If you can't run the project on less than $1 million, that's your bottom line. Rebuff any efforts to drop below the million and walk away if they cannot work with that. This also implies that your opening offer must be higher than $1 million, so you can have the room to negotiate.

- **Offer some trial balloons**

    Until the agreement is signed, you won't have to consider anything as final and binding. Make some suggestions. What if the team could address one feature as Phase One, then work on building additional features in later stages, which would allow you to stay at the $1 million mark?

- **Understand your status**

    As the project manager, you would naturally have a significant status because of your proximity to the project. You may well have more than the other party which you should leverage. You could obtain additional concessions if the other side needs to reach an agreement with you.

- **Consider authority**

    You want to deal with the person who has the authority to make decisions on the other side. Dealing with them directly often means you can reach an agreement quicker.

    Conversely, you may want to send a representative out to negotiate on your behalf. You will have time to review the proposal instead of being pressured into an agreement on the spot, and can counter them where necessary.

- **Don't reward intimidation**

    Set expectations and boundaries; don't let other parties push you back over these lines. You'll probably need to learn how to push back against clients who are unreasonable in terms of scope, budget, time, or all three at once. Once you start allowing them to cross the lines, you're training them to continue to do that. Hold the line.

Achieve More with Negotiation

If you want to improve your negotiation techniques, there are some advanced ones you can use. One characteristic of a good negotiator is having a high level of *emotional intelligence*. Rather than being caught up in the emotions—especially during a stressful negotiation—you can focus on interests rather than positions.

Consider improving the following techniques:

- **Use humor**

    Caveat: if you have a dry or dark sense of humor, this strategy may not work well! However, if you can break the ice and get some smiles out of everyone, you can help them relax. It may lead people to back off the cliff and reconsider their stance.

- **Make the pie bigger**

    This is how you would get to the third win-win alternative. Show the people you're negotiating with that your proposal means everyone gets more. If their goal is to maximize benefits from a deal, they can receive even more from your solution than if they won with their proposal.

- **Don't be afraid to show your strength**

    Negotiation isn't gambling; it's not necessarily a bad idea to be open and show your cards. If you're operating from a position of strength because you have a strong BATNA, they'll stay at the table longer to keep you from walking away, assuming theirs is weaker.

    Plus, if they've prepared as you have, they should know your BATNA and be aware of your strength anyway.

- **Take a break when you need to**

    Sometimes, the right thing to do is call a temporary halt. That doesn't mean the negotiation is over, but it's a good idea to let everyone cool off. Otherwise, you may want some time to process an offer or just go to the bathroom. The point is that you don't have to *literally* sit at the negotiating table until you reach the written agreement.

- **Don't fill the silence**

    This tip is particularly powerful after you've made your proposal. Don't rush to justify, rationalize, or explain; let it sit.

Let them look skeptical and be skeptical while they're chewing it over. You don't have to jump in, and you'll look stronger for being able to sit through the silence.

- **Reframe**

  Try to focus on one or two interests and continue to reframe the conversation around them. Doing so keeps it simple and everyone on track. Make sure you have your goals prepared and continue to bring the discussion back when it meanders. Also, keep the conversation around topics where you would have a higher power.

- **Listen actively**

  Be curious about your negotiation partners. Try to get to know them and their thought processes. Concentrate on what they're saying. You can ask questions to clarify and summarize, which can be used as a mini-close.

  Learn where you share interests; you can use them to build an agreement and show that you're not so far apart that you cannot find a third alternative that will leave both of you better off.

- **Tune into station WII-FM**

  This comes into play a lot as a project leader, doesn't it? In a negotiation, you need to know how your offer will benefit the other party. If it doesn't have value to them, why would they agree to it?

- **Understand all sides**

  To reach your goals, you need to know what they are. If you're not already sure what you want out of the process, spend some time figuring that out before you begin negotiating.

  Know what the others want as well. Is there anything that's not important to you that you could use as a tradeoff to get something

you do want? Understand that going in as well. You might try to discover what's not as important to them, so you'll know how they're using their leverage. What are their interests? What is their BATNA? What is the acceptable minimum?

Facilitation

This is similar to negotiation, in that you are trying to bring something to a successful close. In this case, it may be a meeting or discussion. Empowering your team means discussions, which might be contentious. Ideally, the facilitator is neutral, but that won't always be possible on projects for PMs because you have a significant stake in the outcome.

There are six core competencies to be a successful coordinator in these situations (Adams et al., 2006).[21]

1. Create collaborative relationships with clients

PMs must develop working and fruitful partnerships with their clients.

2. Develop and maintain a participatory environment

This skill comes along with being a high EQ leader. The project leader must demonstrate openness and humility that encourages everyone to participate. They have to manage conflict and promote the creativity of the team members.

3. Plan good group processes

Not only does a PM need to set aside time and a location for the group to collaborate, but also to choose the methods that would foster an inclusive atmosphere and result in high-quality deliverables.

4. Model professional positivity

Project managers need to act with integrity and trust that the group will find their way.

5. Guide the group to a good outcome

This one is pretty self-explanatory. The group needs to reach a consensus on the subject under discussion, and the PM helps to facilitate that.

6. Develop and sustain knowledge of facilitation

Unlike professional facilitators, project managers don't need to achieve certifications in the field and maintain their professional standing in it. However, they should be aware of the vital facilitation methods that would help them achieve their goals.

Facilitate Effective Discussions

As a facilitator, you'll be guiding the team rather than directing it. One of your main tasks will be to keep the discussion on track and target, and there are several ways you can do that.

- **Use agendas and objectives**

    These provide roadmaps for meetings and can help guide discussions. If there's a problem to be solved on the agenda, it's much easier for everyone to focus on it. When the discussion strays, remind everyone that they need to have a solution by the end of the meeting.

- **List action items and their owners**

    To ensure that nothing is left out, you or a notetaker must capture the plan and everyone's responsibilities.

- **Park tangents in the parking lot**

    As you know, it's incredibly easy for a discussion to go off track! People may bring up important issues that need meetings or action plans of their own, so put them on their own list. The ones who brought up the point can see that it won't be ignored forever, which would help them let go of it during the current discussion.

- **Set ground rules**

    Another theme you've probably noticed as you read through the book is the idea of clarity. It's also essential in a meeting to be clear about whatever rules you set forth.

    Maybe one rule is that everyone puts their cellphone in a basket in the middle of the table. Perhaps there's a topic that needs to be hashed out separately or has already been discussed extensively, which you should ask the participants to avoid so they can concentrate on the actual issue.

- **Set time limits (timeboxing)**

    One way to motivate people to come to a conclusion is to tell them they have five minutes to resolve an issue; then the discussion would move on. This helps those who argue for the fun of it to stop doing so and let the team make a decision.

- **Capture ideas and comments as they come up**

    Discussions move fast. Don't assume you'll have time to go back and ask questions because you won't. Capture everything and ask questions if you didn't hear something or still need clarification. It's good to have a notetaker for this task, so you can focus on the discussion and check the notes after the meetings.

Key Takeaways

Facilitation and negotiation are essential skills that a leader must have to complete a project successfully.

- Negotiation is a complex skill requiring several capabilities. It typically takes place in five stages.

- If you're not a good negotiator now, there will be many ways to improve.

- Facilitation empowers your team members to lead meetings and discussions, and you may need to build these skills as well.

In the next chapter, you will learn about the power of service in leadership.

---

[20] https://www.pmi.org/learning/library/negotiating-project-outcomes-develop-skills-6781
[21] https://www.pmi.org/learning/library/project-meeting-facilitator-more-effective-7988

CHAPTER 7

SERVE
FOR
SUCCESS

WE'VE talked a lot about how the command-and-control leadership style isn't used much anymore because it's ineffective. You may have heard of *servant leadership*, where the one who's running the show would consider themselves a servant of those who follow them. The idea is that, by understanding the needs of their followers and empowering them, the leader can accomplish more. Followers are motivated and engaged and believe that their needs are taken into consideration.

Being skilled at listening and having a high level of emotional intelligence, including empathy, are crucial for making everything work.

Active Listening

Listening requires concentration and freedom from distractions, yet so many of us claim to be having conversations with others while we hold our cellphones, alert for any buzz or beep that tells us we have a new email or social media notification.

People believe they can multitask—or listen to what the person is saying and check their email at the same time—but that's far from true. The mind switches rapidly between tasks because it cannot conduct them simultaneously (Hamilton, 2008).[22] This rapid switching fatigues your brain. Not only that, but it means you're missing what the other person is saying. Put your phone away when you're talking to someone and be in the moment with them.

Listen to understand what the other person is saying because you need to know what their problem is. They may be complaining about another team member not pulling their weight, but the real issue could be that they feel overwhelmed by all the work they have to do.

Recall that most of the message is nonverbal. While you're listening to the language they use, also recognize the tone and *body language*. Sometimes, they may be saying one thing, but their tone and nonverbal communication may suggest another. Asking questions will help you get to the bottom of the matter.

"Seek first to understand, then to be understood." —Stephen Covey

When you want to solve a problem, you have to listen first. When someone's talking to you, how would you know their problem if you don't pay attention? If you assume you know what it is because it sounds like a problem you've heard before, your solution won't work.

You didn't define the problem correctly, because you didn't listen to the person actively. If you don't think you understand what they mean, ask more questions and clarify until you can summarize it and they confirm that's the problem.

About 75-90% of a project manager's time is spent in communication (Haus, 2016).[23] Don't worry; we'll get to that topic in more detail in the next chapter. However, that doesn't mean you should be spending all that time talking; you have two ears and one mouth for a reason. Fortunately, active listening is something you can practice anywhere—not just at the worksite. Practice putting your phone down and listening to what your kids, spouse, and friends want to say. You might be surprised how interesting they are when you're not distracted.

Emotional intelligence (EQ)

It's always been important for leaders to have a decent IQ, which measures critical thinking skills. But today's modern business world demands a high EQ as well. When managed effectively, emotions help build interpersonal relationships and create strong bonds that so many people are searching for. It's much more fun and easy to work on a project that you love than one where you're just going through the motions.

You might remember that there are four aspects to emotional intelligence that allow you to develop the environment your team members—and even stakeholders—can thrive in. The good news is that EQ—unlike IQ—is not fixed, and you can work on improving yours.

1. Self-awareness

This includes recognizing and understanding one's own emotions. Build this skill by:

- Naming the emotion.
- Journaling about it.
- Letting your body alert you—for example, many people find their stomach tightening when they're stressed.

2. Emotional management

This is where you would think before you react based on your emotions, as expressing them may be inappropriate at certain times. Build this skill by:

- Taking responsibility for your own life without playing the victim or blaming others.
- Pausing before speaking and asking yourself if what you're about to say is necessary, kind, and true.
- Requesting feedback.
- Finding humor in the situation.

3. Self-motivation

Build this skill by:

- Visualizing success.
- Networking with like-minded people.
- Using positive affirmations.

4. Management of others' emotions

This is also helping them regulate their emotions, so they can be productive. Build this skill by:

- Putting yourself in the other person's shoes.
- Listening without judging or problem solving.
- Modeling how you want others to behave by demonstrating the behavior yourself.

You must start by managing your own emotions before you can move on to helping others. It's like being on an airplane: when the oxygen masks come down, you would put yours on first. That's what enables you to help others.

There are many benefits of having a high EQ as a project leader, particularly in terms of relationships. That would include not only the people on your team but also the client and stakeholders. By understanding your emotions, you give others the space to accept theirs. You'll also accept other people as they are, which will help them to bond with you.

When you can recognize your character and the fact that you make mistakes, it becomes easier for team members to hold themselves accountable for their work. Being open and emotionally honest as the PM gives everyone else the confidence to be honest as well, which is what you need for a well-functioning team unit.

Problem solving relies on all team members being comfortable enough to challenge others and voice their ideas. They need the psychological space to do so, which you can provide as a leader with high EQ. Those who know they won't be shamed for making mistakes or raising unpopular opinions can feel free to brainstorm and own their responsibilities.

Empathy

This is a critical component of having high emotional intelligence: not sympathy, but empathy. Both are useful, but empathy is more important to a PM. Sympathy is when you feel sorry for someone else's misfortune. If the father of one of your team members dies, you would feel sympathy for them.

Sometimes people believe mistakenly that empathy is merely stepping into someone else's shoes, but you're still looking out at the world from your own perspective. Empathy is actually perceiving the world the way someone else would see it—someone with a background, educational achievement, and experiences that are different from yours. This is much harder but more rewarding.

Once you realize where someone's coming from, you can understand better why they're not as enthusiastic about the project as you are, or why they're having more difficulty with something than you had anticipated. It's not a personal vendetta against you or a desire to throw a wrench into the works.

All team members have a life outside of work, as do you hopefully! Such also implies that there will be issues affecting their work in one way or another. As a PM, you must be aware of these, and when you've built connections with team members, they'll let you know what's happening.

There may be times when you need to cut them a break. People aren't robots, and no one can expect them to behave like automatons. An empathetic project leader will understand what's happening and adjust expectations accordingly.

Key Takeaways

Serving your followers is a critical factor in success with modern projects. A project leader with high emotional intelligence is best able to lead their team and have the members motivated and determined enough to achieve their goals.

- Active listening is a critical skill that all PMs need to master, knowing that they must understand the other person first before they can begin to offer solutions.

- High emotional intelligence can be developed and is essential for building relationships with team members, clients, and stakeholders.

- Empathy is a crucial factor in emotional intelligence, and it allows you to see the world from someone else's viewpoint.

In the next chapter, you will learn how to improve your communication.

---

[22] https://www.npr.org/templates/story/story.php?storyId=95256794
[23] https://www.projectmanagement.com/blog-post/18979/Are-Your-Communication-Habits-Good-Enough-

CHAPTER 8

WHAT WE HAVE HERE IS A FAILURE TO COMMUNICATE

WE learn to talk at an early age. Usually, we would start off by making demands, and as we grow older, we develop the ability to hold a conversation. As a project manager, you might have developed some decent communication skills. However, no matter what your starting point is, you can always improve.

Communication seems very simple since most of us have been doing it pretty much our entire lives. We listen when someone else speaks, and when we talk, other people listen—at least in theory. But if it's so easy, why is one of the most common complaints about work life the *lack* of communication?

This topic is particularly critical for project managers because you are the nexus between the client, team, and stakeholders. As a project leader, you need to influence and persuade senior management to endorse and promote the project, get the resources you need from line management, and generate stakeholder support as well. If your communication skills aren't tip-top, you could endanger your own success.

I've led several different projects and initiatives, and I'll tell you the two absolutely necessary elements for being a leader; one is the ability to gather information and understand the situation of the past, where it is now, and where it will be in the future once you have achieved your goals.

The second is to distribute this information clearly and convincingly. Remember that whether you think you can achieve the goal or you cannot, you're right. Everyone around you must understand precisely what you're trying to tell them and believe that you believe it can be done.

Process of Communication

The procedure for interacting with others is simple, which doesn't mean that getting your exact message across will always be easy. There's a sender and a receiver of the message, which may be delivered through different media, such as emails, face-to-face conversations, or online forums.

When you're the receiver, you should be practicing active listening skills, as discussed earlier. Summarize when you think you understand and ask questions when you don't. Once you have agreement from the other person that your summary is exactly what they're trying to get across, you know you haven't misinterpreted anything and can move on.

When you are the sender of the message, though, there's no guarantee that the other person is actively listening to you. They may be waiting for you to hurry up and finish so they can jump in, or they've been

distracted by their cell phone, so they only heard about half of what you were talking about or misunderstood your message.

The context of your message may affect how the other person perceives it. For example, a stakeholder could interpret your words differently from how a team member would. Either of them could interpret your words differently if they experienced a positive life event recently, like getting married, or a negative one like getting divorced. In other words, there are a variety of reasons why your message won't be copied from your thoughts to what the other person understands.

Face-to-face communication contains a lot more information than any other method of transmission. Because digital messages are more limited, they're more likely to be misunderstood. However, you are accountable for the project's results, so it would be in your best interest to ensure that your message is delivered as clearly as possible to minimize misinterpretations, even if the people receiving the message aren't using good listening techniques.

Expectations

One reason why messages could fail is if you don't set expectations. With your project team members, you would set the rules for what would be appropriate. There may be some guidelines that you can expect them to follow absolutely, but for the rest, empower them to get everything done as they see fit.

When you have a team of high achievers, you'll want to reduce the amount of work where you have a procedure for them to follow. Be humble and recognize that they might have a faster or better solution than yours. Consider breaking up large tasks into smaller pieces. Whenever a little goal is achieved, the team member can check off a box and see how far they've progressed.

You need to set expectations with other stakeholders, such as clients and vendors. How often would you sit down for a meeting? Some may be all too eager to block off time on their calendars, whereas others may require your persuasion skills to set regular update meetings. How will they get messages to you and the team? Again, make sure any boundaries or guidelines you're setting are clear, precise, and agreed to with the other party.

Influencing and Persuasion

As a high EQ leader, you already know that you cannot command your project team members like an old-school general. You also understand that you cannot mistreat the client or order them around. For all the people you have relationships with on the project, there will probably be times when you need to convert them to your way of thinking. These are skills that you can develop through practice, both at work and in your personal life. There are several ways to increase your influence as a project manager.

- **Let go of the result**

    Don't spend so much time worrying about whether you'll achieve your goal with communication. You don't have control over whether someone else agrees with you or not. You have control over your message.

    What are the benefits of your suggestion for the other person's organization and for them personally? Take your time exploring that instead.

- **Crowdsource with other PMs**

    Ask colleagues how they would or have handled a similar situation, and what kind of results they got. Have them look over your proposal and decide if they have any suggestions.

- **Create multiple proposals**

    In other words, have a Plan B, and maybe also a Plan C if your first idea doesn't go over well. Someone who didn't like your first suggestion could still be amenable to finding a different solution.

- **Question your assumptions**

    Ask yourself what you're assuming about the person you want to speak with. Are those assumptions valid? Before you make a proposal based on the assumption, ensure that it's right first.

- **Find your weakest link**

    What is the weakest aspect of your proposal? Once you've identified it, see if there's a way you can make it stronger.

- **Always act with integrity**

    As soon as people perceive you as dishonest or acting with a hidden agenda, they will lose trust in you. If they don't trust you, they won't be influenced by you, no matter how much of a smooth talker you are.

Stakeholders

One key communication channel that you will have while on a project is with the stakeholders. You need to keep them apprised of what's going on and enlist their help in various ways to deliver the project successfully. You'll often find yourself using your powers of persuasion with them.

You might recall that a stakeholder is literally anyone who has a *stake* in the project; anyone who is impacted by it. Stakeholders include clients, project team members, colleagues, managers, executives, and suppliers. They may be within the organization that's sponsoring the project or external, such as vendors and regulatory authorities.

If the project doesn't meet the stakeholders' expectations, it could be considered a failure. You need to keep them all in mind. Sometimes, the needs of one group might clash with another. For example, you might be working on a project to bring a new product to your client's market, but the regulatory authorities have some concerns about it.

This would mean that you need to tailor your message to them individually, so they can have the information they need. For example, your discussions with senior executives or high-level officers will typically be at a 30,000-foot height, giving them the highlights of the progress and challenges. They won't have the time to deal with smaller details and mostly prefer a brief summary rather than an in-depth discussion.

By contrast, your talks with the project team about the same subjects could be lengthy. They would require more details than you have considered, so the team would develop an original way to solve it.

Each interaction with a stakeholder is a chance to improve the relationship. Even if you already have a solid bond, there should be no reason not to make it even stronger.

Effective Communication

This is what supports the ultimate project success. When you're communicating with the wrong people, sending incorrect information, too much, or too little, you're decreasing the chances of achieving your goals. It starts with knowledge—who your stakeholders are, what the client's business objectives are, and how the project aligns with them.

Before you get started putting together the plan, it helps to answer the **Five Ws and an H**: Who, What, When, Where, Why, and How.

- **Who** will you be communicating with? In other words, who are your stakeholders?
- **What** is the message? Will you probably have more than one?
- **When** will the message(s) be sent? Like voting, communication should happen early and often.
- **Where** will the messages be disseminated? Online, in person, or both?
- **Why** do the receivers need the message? Remember to tailor it to the person and tell them what the benefit is for them.
- **How** will the message(s) be sent? Email, online forum, in person, one-on-one, town hall, or all of the above?

For communication to be *effective*, it must be the **right message**, sent at the **right time**, to the **right people**, and in the **right way**.

1. Right people

These are the stakeholders, and a vital function for project success is not only to identify all of them but also to determine WII-FM for each of them.

Match KPIs (key performance indicators) for all levels of management. If they're rewarded based on productivity, calculate how much more productive their teams will be once they've implemented the improvement, for example.

Once you know how the project benefits each stakeholder, you can craft your message appropriately.

2. Right way

For each stakeholder and message, consider the best mode of communication. If you have something that needs to be disseminated quickly across the organization, an email could be the best way to get that information across. Newsletters and intranet are similar possibilities.

If the company has a knowledge repository or central data hub, as a project manager, you need to know how it gets updated and by whom.

There are times when collaboration is called for, especially if a decision must be made. Although email has undoubtedly been used in the past—where participants would go back and forth until they reach a resolution—it's inefficient. Face-to-face or virtual meetings over video calls are best for collaboration.

Know whether messages are being sent internally or externally, and you need to be careful when sending them outside the organization. Include nondisclosure agreements, no confidential or intellectual property, and follow the company's guidelines.

Even for internal communications, not all employees will have the same level of knowledge about specific projects and operations. Be careful about what's considered confidential within the firm.

3. Right message

Consider the person that you're communicating with for each message. What is the appropriate level of detail? Bring your empathy to the message and step into their shoes. It's critical for all stakeholders that you consider the information from their viewpoint.

Does this mean that you must craft a separate email for each person you need to communicate with? That's just not realistic, given all other demands on your time. Think about the groups of people who need to get the message similarly instead.

For example, you may be dealing with executives in different departments, but they all just need a summarized update of what's happening. They can get the same email. Likewise, although your team members

are working on different aspects of the project, you can send out one email to all of them with team-specific information.

Templates are also beneficial when you're trying to maximize the time you spend on communications. Have a status report template that you can update and send to all interested parties, for example.

However, not all communication can be satisfied with emails and templates sent to everyone. Sometimes—and especially when you're working with large and mature firms—there will be a central hub where you can keep updates and other information instead.

The key to successful and clear communication is keeping it short and straightforward. No one has the time to read a wall of text these days, so don't send one. Keep your missive objective short, focused on the project, and containing what you want people to know.

When you need to share bad news, don't try to hide it in a thicket of sentences or irrelevant information. Be clear about it and offer solutions without excusing or blaming.

What action do you want the receiver to take upon from the message? If you have a call to action, make it clear what the recipient is intended to do and don't bury it in a tangle or irrelevance either. You may want to separate it visually from the rest of the message to draw their attention to it.

4. Right time

Communication must be frequent so that everyone can have the latest information. You may discuss with your stakeholders how often it would be reasonable for them to hear from you. Be prepared and propose a frequency because stakeholders often rely on you being an expert who knows what's best.

Don't let them demand too much communication that could interfere with the project. On the other hand, monthly or quarterly meetings are not frequent enough when you have decisions to be made weekly.

Automation works well for regular messages, and many project management software applications contain this functionality. In addition to timed messages that occur regularly, you'll also need to deliver them on a more ad-hoc basis, especially in times of crisis or emergency.

How Effective is Your Communication?

It's helpful to measure whether you're getting your message across, so you can fine-tune anything that needs to be adjusted. As a PM, you're not the most objective assessor of the impact of your messages; therefore, you need to ask the recipients for feedback.

- **Regularly**

    When you set the expectation that you want to receive constructive criticism on your communication skills, so you can serve your stakeholders more professionally, it helps them feel better about providing that feedback.

    Feedback isn't a one-and-done type of deal; it should be a loop where you would ask for feedback, receive it, incorporate it, and ask for it again.

- **Ask during meetings**

    Whether in a meeting with your team or one-on-one, you can ask if they're getting the information they need for their job. How can your communication be improved? Is there anything they like or want you to do more of?

- **Ask in your written messages**

    In your emails, you can ask specifically if there is more information they need to make a decision to be more effective in their jobs.

- **Anonymous surveys**

    Sometimes, people are a little reluctant to give direct feedback because it makes them feel like they're attacking the other person, even when they're not. Likewise, people may just be unwilling to give you feedback, especially if you are still working on this aspect of your leadership and tend to get defensive. An anonymous online survey is the easiest way to gather feedback if your requests aren't providing useful information. They're easy to set up, and you can give everyone space to write comments.

- **Listen**

    When people provide feedback, you may want to rationalize, excuse, justify, or blame someone else. Do none of the above. Practice your active listening skills and only speak to clarify or summarize, so you can ensure you understand what they're telling you. Be humble.

Don't forget to incorporate that feedback and let everyone know! You can ask for feedback as much as you want, but if people think you're ignoring it, they won't want to waste their time any longer. Once you have gathered the feedback, implement it. Then, let the stakeholders know what you've done to incorporate what they suggested.

Key Takeaways

In real estate, they always say it's about location, location, location. But in project management, it's about communication, communication, communication.

- There's a communication process that involves the sender, receiver, and message, though it ends up being more complex than that.

- You need to set clear and reasonable expectations for team members and stakeholders.

- PMs must develop their influence and persuasion skills to increase the chances for project success.

- Effective communication involves sending the right **message** at the right **time** in the right **way** to the right **people**.

- Ask for feedback to improve your communication.

In the next chapter, you will learn about essential leadership traits that all PMs must have.

CHAPTER 9

HECG SECRET FOR SUCCESS

AS they used to say in the old TV commercials: *but wait! There's more!* Yes, we have discussed many topics, characteristics, skills, and information that a successful project manager needs to know. However, there are still a handful more, and mastering them will put you on the road to becoming the kind of a leader that you've always wanted to be.

Humility

We've touched on this trait briefly, especially in the section about emotional intelligence. By now, you know that it's necessary to create an open and honest environment that will help you get most out of your project team. When the team leader is humble and admits they don't know everything, it creates space for them and others to make mistakes and learn from them.

You've also discovered that a key factor in leadership is continuous learning and improvement. By definition, if you think you know everything already, you block yourself from learning; if you can't learn, you can't improve. No one human being could possibly know everything there is to comprehend; one look at the Internet can tell you that.

It's essential that you understand what you don't know. Although this is the third book I've written about the various aspects of project management, you can see that there is still more to learn. However, now you have a thorough grounding in the fundamentals and can be confident about going out and building on this new base of knowledge.

You may have heard of the Dunning-Kruger effect or the Dunning-Kruger experiment. Two researchers—David Dunning and Justin Kruger—discovered that people who are incompetent at something generally think they're much greater than they are. Contrarily, those who are actually competent at the same thing usually believe they are less capable than they truly are (Murphy, 2017).[24] This is partially due to humility because competent people understand how much they *don't know* about the chosen topic. You don't want anyone to call you a walking Dunning-Kruger effect because that means you behave like you're much more competent than you actually are!

Other common issues for project managers who aren't appropriately humble include taking unnecessary risks or not planning adequately because they believe they can figure everything out. In this case, they would be focusing on themselves rather than the team or project, not involving enough people in collaboration activities, and concentrating on reputation instead of work or shared values. You probably recognize already that these issues are antithetical to project success and leadership in general.

There are a number of ways you can demonstrate humility and increase the chances for project success at the same time. You can nurture the humble side of your nature as you go through life.

- **Take responsibility**

    Giving up responsibility means losing the power to change the future because the power is given to other people or circumstances; thus, success becomes a matter of sheer luck. You're the one in charge of your life, and humble people own it.

- **Admit when you don't know**

    You know that humility is important and that no one person understands everything about the world. Therefore, admitting that you don't know something is not a badge of shame, but a recognition of reality.

- **Listen and respect others' ideas**

    It's not enough to listen actively, although that is an excellent first step. You also need to avoid dismissing other people's ideas outright. Wouldn't you want to use a great idea to make sure the project is successful, even if it isn't your idea?

- **Show care for your team**

    For a humble leader, followers are valuable, so take care of your team members.

- **Appreciate others' work**

    You might be frugal with your budget, but it's a bad idea to be frugal with praise. If a team member does well, celebrate it. Praise those who make an effort and take time to appreciate everyone's contributions to the project.

- **Be flexible**

    Not only is using agile methodology a good idea but so is being agile with your decisions! Roll with the punches, so your team members can adapt too.

- **Don't micromanage**

    We've discussed how wasteful and unnecessary micromanagement is, and here's another way to look at it: when you're hovering over your team like a helicopter, you're basically telling them you know better than they do, so they must do everything your way.

- **Reflect and improve**

    Even if you are a project manager, you're still human! You'll make mistakes, just as your team will. Take time to look back periodically and think about what went well and what didn't. Use that information to make things better.

Enthusiasm

Consider the people you follow—your mentors or even famous figures that you want to emulate. Are they passionate about what they do? Are they eager to share their knowledge with others? Or are they noncommittal when they talk about what they do?

Right. You want to follow someone who's enthusiastic about their life and the path they've taken. To model this for your team and the other stakeholders, you'll need to discover your motivators.

External motivators like money work for a while, but not for as long as you may think. You'll need to find personal motivation to continue when things get tough. Pride in your work? The satisfaction of tackling a difficult challenge and emerging victorious? Gratification from developing team members into the best people they can be? Feel free to choose more than one and write them down, so you can refer back when times are hard.

Other ways to maintain enthusiasm include getting involved in project management as a profession by giving lectures or teaching. Change things up by volunteering for other projects, either at home or at work. Let go of the things you can't control, so you can focus your energy where you can make a difference.

Composure

As they say, *"Keep calm and carry on."*[25] Projects have a tendency to generate chaos. The larger and more complex—and the more stakeholders you have—the easier it will be for things to spin out of control.

However, as the project leader, you need to stay cool when everything's heating up around you. Model a matter-of-fact approach to problems for your team members and other stakeholders. No matter how much pressure you experience, resist the temptation to dump it onto others' shoulders, particularly your project team.

Another way to handle stress in addition to what was mentioned in Chapter One is to reframe your idea of stress into one of opportunity. Situations that bring additional pressure are often the same ones that would allow you to grow and develop as a person and PM. Look at these events as challenges, where you would have a chance to influence the outcome, then get to problem solving.

Guide

You now know that being a leader also includes being part of the team. You can also think about project leadership as being a guide. Imagine that you're a sherpa taking a group of well-equipped travelers up the mountain. You wouldn't tell them where to put their feet exactly, but you would take them on the trails that you're familiar with. When you get to a fork, you allow travelers to decide which way to go, but you would provide them with your recommendation and the pros and cons of each path if they can't find them.

Sometimes, you will come across a boulder that wasn't in the path before. You clear it away for them or steer them in a path around it. There will be times when the travelers argue about which way to go, and you would be the voice of reason to help them get back to thinking logically through the problem.

When the trail is steep, you would be the one encouraging and motivating everyone to keep going. There will still be times when you need to make an executive decision because the group cannot agree or doesn't have the expertise on the mountain that you do. I think you can see how this fits into your abilities as a project manager.

Key Takeaways

The icing on the project manager sundae is HECG for success: Humility, Enthusiasm, Composure, and Guide.

- Being humble is vital for admitting to your mistakes and learning from those around you, so you can be more successful as a PM.
- People want to follow leaders who are enthusiastic about what they do.
- Stay calm, cool, and collected to help those around you avoid getting caught up in the chaos.
- PMs act as guides for all stakeholders and team members in a project.

---

[24] https://www.forbes.com/sites/markmurphy/2017/01/24/the-dunning-kruger-effect-shows-why-some-people-think-theyre-great-even-when-their-work-is-terrible/#1a8d1f995d7c
[25] https://www.keepcalmandcarryon.com/history/

FINAL WORDS

NOW that you've read through this book, you should have a solid grasp of the kinds of leadership skills that will help you become not just a successful project manager, but also a person with high emotional intelligence. The modern leader empowers and motivates their team members and develops them too.

In previous books, we talked more about the technical skills of project management; but in this one, we focused on leadership, which is almost exclusively about the people. There are various traits that good leaders must have to bring out the best in everyone involved in the project to a successful conclusion and how to deal with common interpersonal problems that arise frequently.

There are many characteristics and skills for a PM to be a successful leader, increasing their ability to become a successful project leader. Problem solving is a key capability, especially when it comes to dealing with issues like politics.

Another crucial skill is conflict management. When you have two or more people in a room or working on a project together, there will be disagreements. Some disagreement is constructive; however, conflicts based on personalities and relationships are typically unhealthy, and the PM needs to work through and eliminate them.

Teams need building and managing. Project managers are responsible for holding the team together through the phases of team building (forming, storming, norming, performing, and adjourning) and hopefully reaching the performing stage, where the team would be acting as a cohesive unit.

Beyond managing the team well, a good project leader will also help develop individual members. This can be done through coaching or mentoring, which is a longer-term process that assists the mentee in developing their career. PMs must understand the people and cultures on their team and delegate to help them grow by taking more challenging assignments.

Negotiation is a life skill that's also particularly critical for project managers. They need to be capable facilitators to help others run meetings and workshops while staying on track.

The idea of servant leadership—or having the leader serve their followers—has grown recently in popularity. To do this properly, the project manager must listen actively and demonstrate high EQ, including empathy, instead of sympathy.

Communication is the lifeblood of any successful project. Being clear and getting one's message across to stakeholders and team members is key to achieving project goals. Communication does involve not only the sender of the message, but also the receiver. PMs need to use their powers of influence and persuasion.

Effective communication involves sending the right message in the right way to the right people at the right time. Project managers can determine whether their communication is effective by requesting feedback. Finally, great project leaders act as guides to everyone involved in the project, demonstrate humility and enthusiasm, and stay calm under pressure.

If you can take only one message away from this book, I hope it's that although there are numerous skills involved in being a leader, all of them can be developed and improved with deliberate practice.

You have everything you need to know to be a *great project leader*. The more you develop your leadership capabilities, the better off you will be in all areas of life. Don't be afraid to make mistakes; just make sure you own and take responsibility for them.

Take everything that you've learned and use it to help you launch a career as a fabulously successful project manager. It's time for you to soar!

REFERENCES

Adams, T., & Means, J. (2006). **The project meeting facilitator.** Project Management Institute. https://www.pmi.org/learning/library/project-meeting-facilitator-more-effective-7988

ASQ. (n.d.). **What is a Fishbone Diagram? Ishikawa Cause & Effect Diagram.** Retrieved from https://asq.org/quality-resources/fishbone

Casper, C. M. (2002). **Using emotional intelligence to improve project performance.** Project Management Institute. https://www.pmi.org/learning/library/emotional-intelligence-improve-project-performance-1019

Center for Creative Leadership. (2020, April 28). **Use Active Listening Skills When Coaching Others.** Retrieved from https://www.ccl.org/articles/leading-effectively-articles/coaching-others-use-active-listening-skills/

Clark, T. (2019, November 11). **9 Tips to Become a More Effective Delegator.** LiquidPlanner. https://www.liquidplanner.com/blog/9-tips-become-effective-delegator/

Cooper, A. (2020, June 23). **Building Your Project Team.** Project Smart. https://www.projectsmart.co.uk/building-your-project-team.php

Covey, S. R. (2013). **The 7 Habits of Highly Effective People: Powerful Lessons in Personal Change.** (Anniversary ed.). Simon & Schuster.

D'Amico, J. (2017, December 7). **Project Management Training Tips: Methods of Persuasion.** American Management Association. https://playbook.amanet.org/training-articles-project-management-tips-persuasion/

Daskal, L. (2018, June 10). **7 Powerful Habits That Make You More Assertive.** Retrieved from https://www.lollydaskal.com/leadership/7-powerful-habits-that-make-you-more-assertive/

Economy, P. (2020, February 6). **5 Remarkably Powerful Ways to Boost Your Confidence.** Retrieved from https://www.inc.com/peter-economy/5-remarkably-powerful-ways-to-boost-your-confidence.html

Englund, R. (2010). **Negotiating for success.** Project Management Institute. https://www.pmi.org/learning/library/negotiating-project-outcomes-develop-skills-6781

Fastenberg, D. (2010, October 18). **Top 10 Worst Bosses.** TIME http://content.time.com/time/specials/packages/article/0,28804,2025898_2025900_2026107,00.html

Goodrich, B. (2019, November 19). **Develop vs Manage Project Team.** PM Learning Solutions. https://www.pmlearningsolutions.com/blog/develop-versus-manage-project-team-pmp-concept-36

Hamilton, J. (2008, October 2). **Think You're Multitasking? Think Again.** NPR. https://choice.npr.org/index.html?origin=https://www.npr.org/templates/story/story.php?storyId=95256794

Harvard Professional Development. (2019, August 26). **How to Improve Your Emotional Intelligence.** Retrieved from https://blog.dce.harvard.edu/professional-development/how-improve-your-emotional-intelligence

Henderson, L. (2018, June 22). **Why Our Brains See the World as "Us" versus "Them."** Scientific American. https://www.scientificamerican.com/article/why-our-brains-see-the-world-as-us-versus-them/

Ikigai Consulting. (2016, August 31). **Humility And Project Management.** Retrieved from https://www.ikigaiconsulting.com/insights/humility-and-project-management

Irwin, B. (2007). **Politics, Leadership, and the Art of Relating To Your Team.** Project Management Institute. https://www.pmi.org/learning/library/politics-leadership-relating-project-team-7276

Keep Calm and Carry On. (n.d.). **History.** Keep Calm and Carry On. https://www.keepcalmandcarryon.com/history/

Levin, G. (2011). **Mentoring—a key competency for program and project professionals.** Project Management Institute. https://www.pmi.org/learning/library/mentoring-key-competency-program-project-professionals-6264

Miller, C. (2016, February 26). **Are Your Communication Habits Good Enough?** Project Management. https://www.projectmanagement.com/blog-post/18979/Are-Your-Communication-Habits-Good-Enough–

Mind Tools. (n.d.). **Boost Your Interpersonal Skills: Building Highly Effective Working Relationships.** Retrieved from https://www.mindtools.com/pages/article/interpersonal-skills.htm

Mind Tools. (n.d.). **Building Self-Confidence: Preparing Yourself for Success.** Retrieved from https://www.mindtools.com/selfconf.html

Morfin, E. (2000). **New Rules for Effective Problem Solving in Projects.** Project Management Institute. https://www.pmi.org/learning/library/appraisal-situation-problem-solving-projects-492

Murphy, M. (2017, January 24). **The Dunning-Kruger Effect Shows Why Some People Think They're Great Even When Their Work Is Terrible.** Forbes. https://www.forbes.com/sites/markmurphy/2017/01/24/the-dunning-kruger-effect-shows-why-some-people-think-theyre-great-even-when-their-work-is-terrible/#1a8d1f995d7c

Nguyen, T. (2014, November 24). **You Don't Say? Body Language Speaks Volumes More Than Words.** Entrepreneur Europe. https://www.entrepreneur.com/article/239831

Ni, P. (2014, October 5). **How to Increase Your Emotional Intelligence - 6 Essentials.** Psychology Today. https://www.psychologytoday.com/us/blog/communication-success/201410/how-increase-your-emotional-intelligence-6-essentials

Obikunle, O. (2002). **Dealing with cultural diversity in project management.** Project Management Institute. https://www.pmi.org/learning/library/dealing-cultural-diversity-project-management-129

Peterka, P. (2019, September 6). **Root Cause Analysis (RCA) for Beginners.** 6Sigma. https://www.6sigma.us/etc/root-cause-analysis-for-beginners/

Planisware. (2020, April 3). **The conflict management guide for project managers.** Retrieved from https://www.planisware.com/hub/blog/conflict-management-guide-project-managers

Project Management Skills. (n.d.). **Problem Solving Techniques & Strategies for Project Managers.** Retrieved from https://www.project-management-skills.com/problem-solving-techniques.html

Psychology Today. (n.d.). **Emotional Intelligence. What Is Emotional Intelligence?** Retrieved from https://www.psychologytoday.com/us/basics/emotional-intelligence

Rajkumar, S. (2010). **Art of communication in project management.** Project Management Institute. https://www.pmi.org/learning/library/effective-communication-better-project-management-6480

Skelsey, D. (n.d.). **10 Most Common Problems In Projects.** Project Laneways. https://www.project-laneways.com.au/blog/articles/10-most-common-problems-in-projects

Stamoulis, D. (n.d.). **Making It To the Top.** Retrieved from https://www.russellreynolds.com/insights/thought-leadership/making-it-to-the-top-nine-attributes-that-differentiate-ceos

Stickney, F., & Johnston, W. (1983). **Delegation and a sharing of authority by the project manager.** Project Management Institute. https://www.pmi.org/learning/library/delegation-sharing-authority-matrix-organizations-1806

Thamhain, H. (2007). **Managing project teams in an age of complexity.** Project Management Institute. https://www.pmi.org/learning/library/managing-project-teams-age-complexity-7212

Toggl. (n.d.). **5 Stages of Team Development.** Retrieved from https://toggl.com/stages-of-team-development/

Villax, C., & Anantatmula, C. (2010). **Understanding and Managing Conflict in a Project Environment.** Project Management Institute. https://www.pmi.org/learning/library/understanding-managing-conflict-resolution-strategies-6484

Wachtel, D. (2020, June 22). **How to Improve Your Negotiation Skills.** Negotiations Experts. https://www.negotiations.com/articles/negotiating-skills/

Wikipedia contributors. (2020, June 29). **Five whys.** Retrieved from https://en.wikipedia.org/wiki/Five_whys

Wikipedia contributors. (2020, June 6). **Trust, but verify.** Retrieved from https://en.wikipedia.org/wiki/Trust,_but_verify

Wilemon, D., & Thamhain, H. (1983). **Team building in project management.** Project Management Institute. https://www.pmi.org/learning/library/team-building-development-project-management-5707

Wilson, F. (2020, April 30). **9 Effective Team Management Techniques for Project Managers.** NTask. https://www.ntaskmanager.com/blog/effective-team-management/

Woods, J., & Abdon, P. (2011). **The project manager as team coach—a plan for success.** Project Management Institute. https://www.pmi.org/learning/library/project-manager-team-coach-plan-success-6251

Wong, J. P. (2007). **Beat the burnout.** Project Management Institute. https://www.pmi.org/learning/library/eight-practices-maintain-project-enthusiasm-4575

GLOSSARY AND ABBREVIATIONS

Active listening: Absorbing what the speaker is saying thoroughly .... ch. 7

Adjourning/mourning: The last stage of a team building .... ch. 4

Assertiveness: Communicating directly and respectfully .... ch. 1

Analysis paralysis: Overthinking; not allowing decision making .... ch. 2

BATNA: Best Alternative To a Negotiated Agreement .... ch. 6

BECC: Bond, Empathize, Connect, and Communicate .... ch. 4

CEO: Chief Executive Officer .... ch. 1

Coachable: A person willing to learn from someone else in a competency .... ch. 5

Coaching: A development method to support in achieving a goal .... ch. 5

Dunning-Kruger effect: Incompetent people think they are great .... ch. 9

EQ: Emotional Intelligence (understanding and managing emotions) .... ch. 7

Emotional Management: Acting rationally, not reacting emotionally .... ch. 7

Empathy: Understanding or feeling what another person is experiencing .... ch. 7

Extrinsic motivators: External motivators, such as salary, bonuses, time off .... ch. 4

Fishbone diagram: Cause and effect or Ishikawa diagram .... ch. 2

Five Ws and an H: Who, What, When, Where, Why, and How .... ch. 8

Five Whys: A root cause analysis framework .... ch. 2

Forming: The first stage of a team building .... ch. 4

Framework: Describes how to achieve a goal following a methodology .... ch. 2

Global project: A project with members in different locations .... ch. 3

Issue log: A list of all issues with their descriptions and statuses .... ch. 4

Intrinsic motivators: Internal motivators, such as being proud, exciting work .... ch. 4

KPIs: Key Performance Indicators .... ch. 8

Leadership: A combination of skills, characteristics, and behaviors .... ch. 1

Mentoring: Guidance by a more experienced person .... ch. 5

Mind Map: Generating and mapping ideas visually .... ch. 2

Nonverbal communication: Tone, speed of speech, body language .... ch. 1

Norming: The third stage of a team building .... ch. 4

Performing: The fourth and desired stage of a team building .... ch. 4

PM: Project Management .... ch. 1

PMI: Project Management Institute .... ch. 2

Sandwich the critique: Positive statements before and after critique .... ch. 4

Self-awareness: Recognizing and understanding their own emotions .... ch. 7

Soft skills: Communication, leadership, and relationship skills .... ch. 5

Stakeholder: Has "stake" in the outcome of the project .... ch. 8

Storming: The second stage of a team building .... ch. 4

Three Ps: Prepared, Positive, and Patient (a negotiation guideline) .... ch. 6

WBS: Work Breakdown Structure (a tree structure with activities) .... ch. 4

WII-FM: What's In It For Me or Them (a way of communication) .... ch. 4

LEAVE A REVIEW

I would be incredibly *thankful* if you could take just 60 seconds to write a brief review on Amazon, even if it's just a few sentences.

If you have downloaded the bonus checklist for getting support from the managers, sponsor and stakeholders (the link is at the beginning of the book), you can attach it to your review and share your experience. This will inspire and encourage other fellow project managers who may have difficulties getting necessary support from their project partners.

Please type this link into your browser or scan the QR code:

amazon.com/dp/B08WRSQWVS

Customer Reviews

 51

4.8 out of 5 stars ▼

5 star		94%
4 star		2%
3 star		0%
2 star		2%
1 star		2%

See all 51 customer reviews ▶

Share your thoughts with other customers

Write a customer review

My Other Books You Will Love

For a complete collection of books, visit the author page

amazon.com/author/rsagile

2-IN-1
THE EFFECTIVE
PROJECT LEADER

2021

www.ingramcontent.com/pod-product-compliance
Lightning Source LLC
Chambersburg PA
CBHW021438070526
44577CB00002B/214